EVERYTHING
IS A BLESSING

TIMELESS WISDOM
FOR A HAPPY LIFE

DAVID VENNELLS

First published by O Books, 2006
An imprint of John Hunt Publishing Ltd., The Bothy, Deershot Lodge,
Park Lane, Ropley, Hants, SO24 0BE, UK
office@johnhunt-publishing.com
www.o-books.net

USA and Canada
NBN
custserv@nbnbooks.com
Tel: 1 800 462 6420 Fax: 1 800 338 4550

Australia
Brumby Books
sales@brumbybooks.com
Tel: 61 3 9761 5535 Fax: 61 3 9761 7095

Singapore
STP
davidbuckland@tlp.com.sg
Tel: 65 6276 Fax: 65 6276 7119

South Africa
Alternative Books
altbook@global.co.za
Tel: 27 011 792 7730 Fax: 27 011 972 7787

Text copyright David Vennells 2006

Design: Stuart Davies
Cover design: Book Design, London

ISBN-13: 978 1 905047 22 2
ISBN-10: 1 905047 22 3

A CIP catalogue record for this book is available from the British Library.

Printed by Maple-Vail, USA

EVERYTHING
IS A BLESSING

TIMELESS WISDOM
FOR A HAPPY LIFE

DAVID VENNELLS

BOOKS

Winchester, UK
Washington, USA

THANKS

Many thanks to everyone who has helped in the making of this book. Especially thanks to John Hunt for being enthusiastic and encouraging about the idea and to Shen Mei for giving me a clear direction and to Eva Pavon for being a great friend and providing constant support.

CONTENTS

INTRODUCTION

The big difficulties in life like serious illness, relationship or money problems can be a real blessing in disguise. Many spiritual traditions teach that we can actually use our problems to facilitate personal and spiritual growth and eventually develop a level of inner happiness and wisdom that is beyond all suffering. This kind of stable inner happiness does not come easily, it has to be worked for and it takes time to develop the inner strength and wisdom to be able to skillfully transform our daily problems into spiritual growth. But genuine inner happiness is something worth striving for and something that will last way beyond this life. If you try to put the techniques described in the book into practice on a day to day basis at the very least you will become happier, more content and better able to deal with the pressures of daily life and hopefully over time you will also become a kinder and wiser human being, something that our world really needs.

I have tried to make this book as practical as possible. There is a brief summary at the end of each chapter together with a relevant exercise and meditation and a blank page to make some personal notes. One way to really use these 'extras' effectively is to just read one chapter per week, but read it two or three times and make some notes on the blank page about the things that are really useful and relevant to your life and try to apply any techniques or wisdom from that chapter throughout the week. Also read through your own notes and do the meditation every day if you have time, even just a few minutes of meditation can make a big difference to your day. Another method would be to read the whole book first and then re-read it more slowly and methodically and again try to use the exercises, techniques and meditations. Do whatever works for you! I have also highlighted certain phrases throughout the book that might be helpful for reflection or meditation. If you find yourself lacking enthusiasm just flick through the book, choose a phrase that hits the spot and go meditate, discuss it with someone or just go for a walk and chew it over, eventually your mind will change!

Use this book to create your own detailed plan for personal growth and inner transformation. I can only make suggestions based on my own and others' experience, make your own mind up and only use the techniques and ideas that you think will really produce results for you. If you just read this book like a normal book after a few weeks you will have forgotten most of the good advice and no lasting change will have occurred. Treat it more like a course of study, make lots of notes about what you think could be really helpful and develop your own ideas from these. Don't think of it as academic study but treat it as a new beginning and enjoy the exciting process of planning your journey of spiritual and personal growth. Hopefully by the end of the book you will have developed a plan for inner change that you can realistically apply to everyday life and that can be developed as the months and years go by. This way lasting inner change is within your reach.

This book contains a combination of some of the techniques I have learnt from Buddhism, personal experience and advice from friends and teachers. I can only say that if you sincerely apply some of these ideas to your life for a few months and see what impact it has on your quality of life then you will also know from your own experience what the future might hold if you continue to develop your mind. This is not a book about Buddhism because I am not qualified to write one, so if you find some of the ideas helpful try reading an authentic text, see appendix 2.

Wishing you good health and great happiness.

If you want to know more about the author visit www.healingbooks.co.uk

1

TURNING AROUND

After reading this chapter you should be able to:

Examine your life in a new light

Know why it is important to look for happiness in the right place

Feel that your future can be much better than your past

This book could seriously damage your problems, this book could destroy your unhappiness, this book could stop your suffering forever, are you ready? I am joking, well half joking! But I couldn't resist a start like this, because in one sense it sounds like the most superficial kind of sales talk. We are so used to the hollow pitch of advertising promising us heaven on earth that we immediately switch off when we hear something like this. But perhaps this is a good sign, perhaps we are developing some wisdom to see what is genuine and will lead to happiness and what is false and will lead to disappointment. *Increased cynicism of a selfish and materialistic approach to life must be the sign of a healthy mind.*

I find this kind of start particularly amusing because in my heart I know it is true. This book can be one of your first steps to a place where all your problems are solved where there is no suffering only peace, understanding and happiness. Does this sound ridiculous? It probably does, I think a part of me thinks that too. That stubborn, proud, intellectual, egotistic and selfish part of my mind doesn't even want to go there, because it means that part of my mind must die as part of the path to lasting happiness. I do feel a little closer to that special place now than I was a few years ago and I think I have met people who are there all the time. Their world is not a heavy world like ours, their world is full of kindness and purpose, they experience a perfect quality of inner peace and mental clarity that is beyond our understanding. We do not need to die to experience this, we do not need to leave the material world and escape to a mountain retreat and engage in years of strict meditation. That path is right for some but not for the majority of people nowadays. There is another path that is perfect for our time and for our type of 'modern' mind.

Once when I was in the middle of a long illness and feeling very low a friend said to me 'everything is a blessing'. What bad advice I thought, some friend! What I wanted was for him to listen to me and let me get things off my chest, but 'everything is a blessing' what does that mean? This wound me up so much that I couldn't get his words out of my mind for hours, I completely forgot about being ill and feeling sorry for myself! Because my mind was taken off the problem the problem ceased to exist. It occurred to me after a while that his words, although seemingly inappropriate, were a blessing. I began to think that if I could do that myself if I could take my own mind off my problems and maybe even see problems as blessings to be 'unlocked' then this would be a very wise way to live.

Normally we try to avoid problems but they can be so useful. In this case it was the illness and the seemingly bad advice that helped me to become a little wiser and happier. *Wise people take every opportunity to learn and grow and consequently over the course of their lives they become happier and stronger and deeper and freer*

beings. Yet for the rest of us we seem to keep making the same mistakes. Life seems to take its toll, it depletes our enthusiasm, robs us of our youth and makes us cynical and uncaring. Yet all we have to do is change our attitude and this will transform our life. If we can start to see problems, like illness or difficult relationships or any challenge you can imagine, in a new light they can become real stepping stones along the path toward fulfilling our unique human potential.

Think of all the things you put your time and effort into, things like your career, making money, education, social life, shopping, entertainment, relationships etc. Can you imagine what would happen if you put all this time and effort into changing your attitude? What would happen to your life if you decided that changing your outlook was a serious and important project that needed a lot of thought, planning, energy, enthusiasm, commitment and action? Of course everything about your life would be completely transformed for the better.

If you decide to improve yourself what will happen? You will improve! If we don't do something radical like this it is foolish to expect our life will improve if we carry on in the same way. I am not suggesting that we should stop shopping or enjoying relationships or striving to improve our career, we just need to be practical and reprioritize our life so that the amount of energy we expend on trying to find some fulfillment and happiness is not wasted by looking for it in the wrong place!

We all want to be happy but we need to start to look within because what we wish for does not exist outside of our mind. Although we probably accept this, in our hearts we do not believe it, we still feel that we will be happy if we have the new car or the new job or the new partner. But the happiness that comes from possessing these things is short-lived and quite shallow. We need to look for happiness in the right place!

I am a slow learner, after studying and even teaching these ideas for many years I keep making mistakes and finding myself back at the start. So on a personal level I hope that writing this book will also help me re-motivate myself and clarify my hopes and intentions for my own inner development. From one point of view I am well qualified to write this book, from bitter experience I know how not to find happiness so I can tell you where not to look! Sometimes I do get things right so I also know a little from experience the right direction we need to take, but you will probably reach the end of this special path before me! It is encouraging to think that a fool can become a wise person but a wise person can never become a fool. To recognize that we have been a fool takes much courage and honesty, but it is such a breakthrough, it is a special realization that can mark a significant turning point in our life.

I would like this to be the sort of book I would have found fascinating and helpful when I was really in need of strength, answers and support, a book that would have pulled me out of myself and pointed me in a new direction toward healing and wholeness when my body and mind were shattered by illness. Long-term illness or any of life's serious difficulties can be very depleting in many ways and we need to be creative and always looking for opportunities to uplift and reaffirm our wish to transform 'problems' into a meaningful experiences, otherwise we just lose our way and life destroys us. *Don't let life get the better of you, use life, whatever it throws at you, to become a better person.*

About fifteen years ago I contracted glandular fever whilst at university, it is a common illness amongst students. My GP told me about one third of all university students contract glandular fever whilst studying for their degree, although in most the symptoms are only as severe as a bad cold and a full recovery is usually made within weeks. My symptoms were quite severe but I wasn't particularly worried as I expected, like all my previous colds and viruses, it would go away. But it didn't and after six months of continuous flu-like symptoms I finally received a diagnosis of ME or Chronic Fatigue Syndrome. ME can be an incredibly debilitating disease and for a young man on the verge of physical, emotional and financial independence this was a huge challenge to face. I struggled through my final year at university putting the little energy I had into my studies but feeling all the time swamped by more and more work and less and less energy. I seemed to spend my whole time either sleeping or studying. Finally I gave in to the illness and stopped studying about two months before my final exams knowing that it was impossible to continue.

I was so ill that my parents had to look after me, I couldn't shop or cook and often I couldn't even get downstairs, they would even wash my hair when my arms were too weak. All this was too much of a challenge and after two years of severe physical illness I succumbed to a period of clinical depression brought on by the stress of being constantly ill. I think this must have been the darkest time in my life, when I was at my worst I would lose days in a blank void of what seemed like almost nonexistence or nothingness. When I wasn't experiencing this I would be in a constant state of anxiety and insomnia with uncontrolled thoughts and emotions coming and going. I felt like my life had been completely destroyed by my illness which was not improving and it seemed like I was in an unending prison. Although I never contemplated suicide my mother later told me that she thought I might try and often worried what she might find when she returned from work. I recently looked through some of the diaries I kept during those times and now it seems like another lifetime. I have almost forgotten how unhappy I was. My life is so different now my physical health has much improved although I am still not able to walk more than a few miles, but I am able to drive, and read and study and shop and look after myself. But the external changes are not the main changes and I think they have come about mainly because of the internal changes.

Internal change is what this book is about and internal change is really what life is about. Although I experience the normal ups and downs of everyday life I often feel more peaceful, relaxed and happy than ever, sometimes I feel that I am very slowly coming to understand myself and life, why we are here and what our potential is. The things that I am beginning to experience and discover now are a direct result of my illness. Without my illness my life would have been more superficial and shallow, without direction or meaning.

The first five years of my illness were the worst. This was partly because my physical condition was at its worst but mainly because I had no idea how to cope with it. At school I had been taught how to read and write, I developed artistic skills and learned sports and computing and many other things like all children. I was taught that accumulating wealth and status and developing a career should be high on my list of priorities. But no one ever taught me how to be happy, how to be content or how to deal with difficult situations like illness. If you ask any parent what they would wish for their children they would always say 'I would like them to be healthy and happy'. *We cannot always expect to find good health or wealth but we can always learn how to develop lasting happiness from within.* This is what we need to teach our children in schools as well as the ordinary things. Our education needs to be useful for life and help us to make the most out of life. At school I wish I had been taught how to relate to others, how to listen to others, how to support others, how to cope with difficult situations and people, how to accept difficult situations that cannot be changed, how to lose, how to cope with stress, how to be confident and positive, how to develop my intuition and inner strength and many other skills that I am only now just starting to develop. What an amazing world this would be if all human beings had this kind of education; a new age of human evolution would begin. Instead we pass on our hang-ups to our children generation after generation.

Towards the end of the worst years of my illness I began to read some books about developing a positive attitude and different kinds of new age thinking. Being ill, although difficult because of my physical suffering, was also a time of discovery. I had been brought up as a Christian and had never been aware of other ways of viewing spirituality, like many people I turned to God only when things became difficult and I lived and planned my life around my own wishes and hopes, never really finding the time, space or inner peace to ask God 'what should I do with my life?' Looking back now I can see my illness as a gift that redirected my life in a very positive direction. Although my life was not negative, just ordinary, spiritually I was going nowhere. *Unexpected problems can be a wake-up call, a chance to start again and begin a spiritual journey, to find out what life was about, to find some meaning and direction.*

Shortly before my long illness began I nearly drowned whilst on holiday in Portugal. I had been swimming in the sea for about half an hour when I heard some shouting. I turned around and saw two people further away from the shore and waving at me. It was a young woman and her elderly father and they were obviously in a state of panic. The elderly man couldn't keep himself above the water. I swam out to them and told the young woman to swim to the shore and alert the lifeguard while I tried to help her farther stay afloat. After a while I realized that I was getting very tired and the tide had turned and was taking us both out to sea. The old man began to panic more and to stay afloat tried to hold on to me so pushing me under the water. As I came up for air I looked back at the shore and could see the old man's daughter standing by the lifeguard station, which was empty! I had absolutely no doubt that this could be the end, I think we both realized this at the same time and stopped struggling. I suddenly felt very peaceful and relaxed and accepting of the situation, and time seemed to slow down. I am not sure what happened next but I soon felt sand beneath my feet and then we were both staggering out of the waves, exhausted and with a stomach full of salt water but very relieved.

A few weeks after I arrived home a friend took me to see a fortune teller, mainly I went just out of curiosity and to please my friend, but I was very impressed with the accuracy of her knowledge about my life and in particular she helped me to identify and articulate something that I had been avoiding in my mind since nearly drowning, mainly that 'I had been given a second chance but things were going to get worse before they got better'! A few months later I contracted the glandular fever which lead to the ME.

Unfortunately it is never over until it's over! During the last six months whilst writing this book I have had more challenging health problems which are still ongoing, nothing life threatening but uncomfortable enough for me to know that some days my mind is still easily upset by small problems and I am still just at the start of the spiritual path. In fact over the last six months my life has fallen apart again, I have had to give up teaching and studying and working, a long-term relationship has come to an end and my body is uncomfortable with illness. But things are much different now than the first time around, now I know that if I try hard and don't worry too much I can accept and transform difficulties into opportunities. *The days when we have the wisdom and the drive to see 'everything as a blessing' are always the most rewarding and satisfying.*

In some ways people who have an easy life are the most unfortunate, they never have the challenges that we need to grow, they never need to reach down inside themselves to find the new qualities and strengths needed to survive and flourish in a challenging world. There is no doubt that there is something special in all of us, and sometimes it needs something life-changing and even life-threatening to shatter our complacency and give us a glimpse of what we can be. If we miss the opportunities to grow life will keep throwing bigger and bigger 'wake up' calls at us. Now is the time to change, now is the time to wake up to a new way of living, stop following everyone else, they are wrong! You know what you have to do, your heart is telling you. The opportunity to become a better person is with us every day. We always have a chance to start again whatever has happened to us or whatever way we have lived our life. Now it is up to you.

The essential points from this chapter are:

You are in a unique position to change your life, if you really want to make a change no one and nothing can stop you. Illness and other problems are only problems if we allow our mind to see them in that way. From another point of view they are exactly what we need to grow.

Exercise:

Write an essay about your own life, be honest, put down in writing all the things that you think have shaped your character and made you who you are today. The objective is to get a clear picture of what has happened to you, who and where you are now and your wishes for the rest of this life and maybe beyond! This can form the beginnings of a life plan, without some kind of plan it is difficult to make significant progress in any direction.

Now try a meditation:

When your mind has settled down develop a good intention like 'may every living being benefit from this meditation'. Spend a few minutes doing the gentle breathing meditation explained in chapter 4. Then meditate using the following contemplation:

Bring to mind a few of the major events and people that have shaped your personality. Just bring them to mind without getting too caught up in your emotions, try to understand how you have been affected by these things, without being judgmental on yourself or others. When you are ready come to a positive conclusion like 'I understand and accept how things have happened', concentrate on this thought until it leaves a deep feeling of acceptance in your mind.

When you have finished make a short dedication like 'through the power of these positive thoughts may all living beings find lasting happiness' and try to carry your positive thoughts into the rest of the day.

Use this page to make some notes on what you found thought-provoking or useful in this chapter:

2

EVERYTHING BEGINS WITH A WISH

After reading this chapter you should be able to:
Develop a clear and deep wish to change for the better
Understand the basic process of training your mind
Begin to regard problems as opportunities for inner growth

I remember wondering many times, as I grew up, what life was about. Why do we exist, is there a meaning to life, why do some people suffer so much? Especially as a teenager I remember spending many hours talking with close friends about these subjects. We had the questions and the curiosity but we had no one to turn to for answers, so we grew up, entered the adult world and began to lose our yearning for understanding. This must happen to so many people, but without a wish to find some meaning and understanding we will not discover anything or grow in any way. So this should be our starting point: we need to recapture some of our wonder and curiosity about life. *We need a strong wish to find a way to overcome our problems and find meaning in life otherwise nothing will change.*

Everything begins in the mind with a wish. All the great achievements of humankind began with a wish. Columbus had a wish to discover a new world and he did, although many thought it impossible. We had a wish to walk on the moon and one day we did, although many thought it impossible. Great buildings begin their life in the mind of the architect, advances in medical science begin in the minds of doctors or scientists. Acts of cruelty come from an angry mind and great acts of kindness come from a compassionate mind. Whatever we do with the rest of our life will begin with a wish in our mind.

If our wishes are ordinary we will achieve ordinary results, if our wishes and dreams are special we will achieve extraordinary results. This simple choice can determine a complete change of life. It takes a real pioneering spirit and a lot of courage to dream of and begin a new way of life in a very ordinary world. Often our environment and the people around us have a huge influence on the way we see ourselves and the way we feel we ought to live. By the time we reach adulthood it can feel that our character is set and change is at best difficult and at worst impossible. Other people become used to the type of person we are and they reflect our self-image making the possibility of personal and spiritual transformation more remote. Often we need a life-changing event, perhaps in the form of illness or bereavement, to glimpse the possibility of change. These initially traumatic events can help us to break the mold or shell that we have created and can help us toward a richer life. *Difficult situations can become meaningful when we have the wish and the wisdom to transform them into learning experiences.*

In my own experience of illness it often seemed there was no great purpose, just suffering and if we look around the world we see people experiencing all kinds of extreme difficulties like famine, poverty and war. Human and especially animal lives are often short, painful and bleak. Many people might disagree but suffering can be more meaningful than success. It can make us more mature, stronger, more empathic and compassionate toward others, more humble and less proud. Fame, money and success can often just feed our ego making us feel superior and creating a childish and selfish mental state. If this were not true all rich and famous people would be deeply happy!

When I began to read books that encouraged a positive approach to illness I became inspired to change my attitude. However I often found that progress was sporadic, two steps forward and one back, and with no clear direction, but at least I felt I had made a start. After a while I realized that what I really needed was clear guidance, a clearly explained path that would take me step by step away from suffering toward a stable and lasting sense of happiness and inner peace. I knew this might not be easy and would involve a certain amount of discipline and hard work but if I found such a path I could work my way along it at my own pace, not expecting dramatic results in one week but just gradually enjoying progress over the rest of my life, maybe over many lives.

After about five years of illness I was introduced to a Tibetan Buddhist teacher who seemed to be a very special example of what a human being could become. His teachings were clear and practical and his presentation and example were completely inspiring. Although I had read some books on Buddhism and felt completely happy with this spiritual approach to life for some reason it had not struck me that this might be the path for me. But listening to this teacher made a huge difference. It seemed from his teachings that we can become a special almost holy being in this life. By following a simple step-by-step approach we can reach a level of consciousness or state of mind that is beyond suffering and we can do this with a special motivation to benefit others that brings great positive energy in to our world. The main message I was getting was that 'we can solve our problems and we can make a difference to our world and this is how you do it'. No one had ever promised me this before so I could not resist the challenge of checking this out for myself!

Human beings have such a special opportunity to do good, to lead a good life, to learn, to grow, to become something special it doesn't have to take millions of years for us, we can evolve in our own life time because we have free will and choice. Unfortunately most of us live our lives in a very small way, we try to gain wealth, popularity, recognition, we build homes and raise families and by the end of our life often our mind has degenerated rather than grown in wisdom and understanding. Children especially need to know they have a special opportunity to develop and grow, a chance to discover the secrets of the universe from within their own mind. If we teach our children to put all their effort in to developing the external world we will not solve the problems of this world and human beings will never evolve beyond our present limited state.

As adults we need to start again, to try to view our life from a fresh perspective. Look at where we have gone wrong and gradually try to live our life as we would like our children or the future people of this world to live. As individuals we have huge power to touch the lives of others if we live in a special way, especially if we have a difficult illness or disability to live with. If other people see us living in a kind and positive way despite our difficult circumstances this can be so inspiring. We have the power to change the future of this world by living in a relaxed and positive way, and always looking for and enjoying opportunities to grow and learn and develop our mind. This way of living is special if we do it for our own good so we can experience some inner peace and personal growth but it is especially powerful if our motivation is to benefit others. *If we try to feel that all human beings are part of our family and their happiness is our responsibility this is a very mature way to live, a sign that we have the beginnings of a great, wise and compassionate nature.*

Even if we cannot honestly live like this every day we can keep it as an ideal to aim for in the future, because if we cannot even imagine the kind of person we want to become we will never achieve it. At some point we have to use our imagination to create a blueprint in our mind for the type of person we would like to become in the future. In Buddhism it is said that of all the countless worlds and universes and types of living beings that exist a human life is one of the rarest and most difficult to obtain, it is even rarer to be human and to have an interest in the spiritual path and then even rarer to find an authentic spiritual teacher. If this is true we have no time to waste!

No matter how old we are we can begin this special journey now, in fact if we are older because of our life experience we can learn deep lessons more swiftly because we understand failure and success, happiness and suffering. Whatever strong habits we die with shape our personality in the next life. If we end our life on a high, spending time developing our understanding and experience of the spiritual path, this tendency will carry us forward to a life of spiritual growth. If we have a positive and flexible outlook and try to make the most of life it is easy to die and let go of this life because we have no regrets. A happy death is a great achievement.

Youth is a state of mind. Some old people have a very youthful heart and many young people grow old before their time, often due to a childhood full of trauma. But if we have a little wisdom we can use whatever difficulties we encounter in life to become stronger, kinder, wiser people. Although often it is trauma and pain that make us feel old if we learn a new approach to life these same conditions can be the cause of eternal youth. Keep wondering, keep young, always feel new, try to develop a happy flexible mind, let go of things when it is time to let go and always try to benefit others. *It's when we let our mind get heavy and we think too much about our own suffering and happiness that our mind gets small and life gets tough.*

Often people with serious illness feel that life has let them down but ironically we might be the lucky ones, we can be like pioneers on the verge of a new world. Man will go further in to outer space but this is not the final frontier. We will not solve the problems of humankind or realize our potential for infinite happiness out there. We must journey within. Buddha said that 'illness has many good qualities'. Initially this seems like a strange point of view as we all wish to avoid illness and any kind of suffering but hard times are never wasted time if we know how to transform them.

We need a strong mind to be able to deal with very challenging situations and come out the other side a more whole and healthy human being. A strong mind means it possesses qualities like flexibility, happiness, peacefulness, patience, understanding and wisdom. But we can only develop these qualities by gradually learning to embrace and use challenging situations to power our personal and spiritual growth. A mountaineer cannot climb without the mountain! Although the mountain causes great hardship to the climber, sometimes even injury and death, because she views the mountain as an opportunity it actually becomes the main cause of her success. The sight of the mountain drives her desire to succeed. If we want to grow, we need a mountain. Illness, difficult people, poverty, failure or any other difficult aspect of our life can provide us with perfect conditions for growth giving us the chance to realize our special inner potential. Whatever is making us unhappy can be transformed in to the main cause of our happiness, just by changing our attitude!

What is spiritual growth? It is about inner transformation, becoming a different person, changing our attitude, transforming our world by transforming our mind. It does take time and effort to change on a deep level so like a mountaineer we have to be practical, we have to train gradually and steadily, we have to learn to conquer small mountains before we can move on to the larger ones. But we can sometimes make big advances quite quickly simply by learning some simple techniques to change our view of our situation. For example, think of something you are having difficulty with at the moment, it might be an illness, a relationship problem, a problem at work. Find a few minutes to sit down and relax or go for a walk in a quiet environment, bring all of the aspects of this difficult situation to mind. As soon as you start to think or feel negatively slowly repeat to your self 'this situation is a mountain, it is an opportunity to grow' or use a similar phrase that works for you. After a while you will notice a positive attitude start to grow in your mind. You have created a new mental environment. Now you know from your own experience that you can change, this might be a very small and fragile start but it can feel very encouraging. From this experience it doesn't take much to realize that if small inner changes are possible in the short term then so are big ones in the long term, all that is needed is commitment and over time we can develop that as well.

The next step is to try to 'hold' the positive attitude you have created. If you lose it repeat the process until it returns. Do this often enough and you will eventually find yourself reacting to problems in a new and positive way. Just through the power of familiarity you will start to view all challenging situations as part of your mountain. *Try to feel that life is a series of mountains to conquer; this feeling will inspire you to take every opportunity to grow.* One of the main obstacles to a happy life is that we see difficult situations and people as just that. If we train ourselves to look beyond this limited perspective we open up a whole new world.

Every time we choose to go in a more positive direction we are doing something very special with our mind. The processes of watching our mind, spotting negative thoughts or emotions at the earliest possible moment, not following these negative patterns, and actively developing positive thoughts and feelings is the process of successful mind training.

Memorize the four steps of mind training:

Watch   Identify   Let go   Live

Eventually the process of reprogramming our mind will become smooth and natural but to begin with it is useful to be aware of these four stages. To begin we need to WATCH our mind just by being aware of our thoughts and emotions in different situations throughout the day. By doing this it is easy to IDENTIFY uncomfortable or negative thoughts as soon as they arise and hopefully before they get a strong hold over us. The sooner we spot or identify negative thoughts or emotions the easier it is to LET GO. If it is too late to let go just walk away from the situation if you can, or distract yourself with something else so that your mind is not being allowed to follow the negative path. Finally if we can we replace the negative with a positive and LIVE. I called the last stage 'live' because positive thoughts and emotions are life affirming, healing and mind expanding.

But don't become too obsessed with this practice. If you overdo it now it is easy to become tired and our training needs to feel enjoyable, gradual and natural if it is going to be continuous and successful. If you want to begin some kind of gentle training today, start by watching your own mind but again not obsessively or constantly, just naturally. Now and then think, 'how do I feel, how are my thought patterns today?' without being hard or judgmental, just watch your mind and develop some self-awareness. Then if you feel ready let go of any negative feelings and repeat some positive words to yourself like 'always rely on a happy mind' or 'may everyone be happy' or whatever feels right for you. Start slowly and when you are ready develop a gentle daily routine for training your mind in this way. This gentle but constant approach builds firm foundations for long-term change and growth.

When we are going through a difficult time in our life we often dream about what we would do if things were different and dwell on how lucky others are. Many people who are healthy or materially fortunate have no real appreciation of their freedom and good fortune. Illness and other problems can seem like a prison and good health and wealth the cause of real freedom and happiness. It seems on the surface that good health and money are a definite cause of happiness and illness and poverty a cause of depression and mental torment. But if this is a universal truth everyone who had a healthy body and lots of money would always be happy and everyone who suffered illness and poverty would be miserable. But we know this is not true. It can take a long time to really appreciate the depths of this truth but our personal happiness, although influenced by external conditions like illness, is really completely dependent on our mind. It is possible to be physically very ill but to have a positive and peaceful mind.

Take some time to think about this carefully, do you accept this truth? If you do then you have to accept that to fulfill your wish to be happy and free from suffering you must learn to develop a happy mind. Also if illness or poverty can be one of the conditions for this to happen you might be more fortunate than a rich and healthy person! Although they are enjoyable we do not actually need good health, wealth, relationships etc. *All we need is a happy mind.* This is a great affirmation to use when you are feeling that the world is against you, just think over and over 'all I need is a happy mind' and slowly you will start to feel the truth of this. Of course we shouldn't abandon money, friends and health, there is no need to and if we did we would be very unhappy and so would others. It takes time to change on a deep level so we have to accept that we will still need the temporary happiness we get from money and relationships until we are strong enough within to really let go. Training the mind is an internal path so we do not need to change our external world too much. Eventually we will be able to let go of these things in our mind, whilst still being surrounded by them and living a normal life. This is important if we want to help others do the same.

We are very influenced by our external world because we are so familiar with it. We spend all our time wrapped up in the external world to the extent that we have almost forgotten that we have an internal world. From the moment we wake up to the moment we go to sleep we are generally completely absorbed in the business of everyday life. *It is very easy to go through the whole of our life without ever spending time getting to know our own mind, yet this is where the answer to all our problems can be found.* In some ways having an illness or other kind of challenging difficulty can be very helpful, these things can help us to stop and think. We often need something or someone to help us take a fresh look at life, if we are not going in the right direction the kindest thing someone can do is to tell us and point us in the right direction. In this sense problems might be our best friend.

When we have a problem in life we tend to solve it by changing something outside our own mind. When we have problems with our partner, friends, career we think of looking for new ones. We are never satisfied for long, we always need new things in our life to keep our sense of well being. Consequently our mind is very discontent and dependent upon good external conditions and we experience very little natural happiness from within. We are always looking for happiness outside of our mind, yet happiness is simply a state of mind. I can't repeat this enough! If we knew how to find inner happiness and 'stay with it' we would not need to put so much time and energy into arranging our external world in such away that we occasionally find some fleeting pleasure.

Illness or any problem can be an opportunity to begin a new way of life. If we always get what we want when we want it we might easily become a very spoilt, shallow and superficial person. Often we need challenges and difficulties to help us grow, to help us become more whole and complete human beings. The big and little problems that come our way can be a great challenge to overcome and can really help us to develop special inner qualities. If we ask our self what is the real meaning of a human life we have to finally say that if we leave this world a better person than when we entered it and if we have helped others to change and grow then our life has had been well lived. If we just accumulated wealth or followed our own selfish wishes what use is this? If this life was just a 'one off', if at the moment of death we ceased to exist then may be we could justify a selfish approach to life. But our mind and our body are different entities when the body dies the mind does not cease because it is not produced from the body, in fact Buddhists believe that the body is produced from the mind! According to the law of Karma the body we have now is the result of our actions in previous lives. Positive actions bring positive results; if we have a healthy body this is good karma returning to us created by our previous positive actions. Our mind is not a physical phenomena like the body, it has no form or shape or color or taste, although it changes in character and ability from life to life, again according to our karma. We know that animals have a mind but it is less intelligent than most human minds. From the Buddhist perspective this is because animals are again experiencing the results of karma, but this doesn't last forever, when their animal karma comes to an end they die and new karma carries them to a new existence in a new body.

Obviously we will not all feel comfortable with this explanation of the different forms of life that exist but I mention it here because understanding the law of Karma helps Buddhists train their mind. If we feel deeply that our words, thoughts and actions shape our future beyond this life we are going to be very careful how we live and how we treat others. If we know that swatting a fly or physically harming others may make us experience poor health in our next life we will let the fly live. In fact if we just consider that a fly has a mind and although quite limited in its mental capacity it can still experience pain this understanding will prevent us bringing more pain in to the world. If we are aware that anger is a cause of ugliness and patience a cause of beauty this will also help to change our behavior.

So in conclusion everyone wants to be happy, even flies in their own way, and in this sense we are all the same, we never wish for suffering. So the real purpose of life is to fulfill this wish and find a pure happiness that never ends and to help others find this. You can find this, many people have, and your problems can help you!

The essential points from this chapter are:

Without a consistent wish nothing will change. Keep developing your wish and your power to change will get stronger. Develop your ability to watch your own mind and identify clearly which are positive and beneficial thoughts and feelings and which are negative and harmful to yourself and others. If we can learn to let go of negative thoughts and feelings and develop positive ones over time our mind will become very peaceful, strong and happy. Eventually even the most difficult situation will not disturb our sense of inner peace.

Exercise:

Develop a realistic plan for learning to watch your own mind. Start in a small way, but be consistent and remind yourself that this is important for your personal happiness. Maybe just begin with half an hour per day. When the time comes, just remember why you are doing this, the more you become aware of what thoughts and feelings are running through your mind the easier it will become to identify which are good and which are harming your happiness. It doesn't matter if you cannot change your mind at this stage, just be gentle with yourself, your ability to change your mind will come in time. Don't change your daily routine, choose the same time every day for mind watching and try to do it whether you are talking, driving, working or whatever. Don't over concentrate, just at the back of your mind try to be gently aware of whether your words, actions, thoughts and feelings are positive or negative. Don't be hard or judgmental, just watch and accept and continue to act naturally. Obviously if you suddenly feel you want to think or talk in a more positive way follow this positive notion! You could also keep a simple diary of your experiences. This can help you to identify more clearly your mental habits and areas that you might like to improve in time.

Now try a meditation:

When your mind has settled down develop a good intention like 'may every living being benefit from this meditation'. Spend a few minutes doing the gentle breathing meditation explained in chapter 4. Then meditate using the following contemplation:

We need to develop the consistent wish to change. Think about how your life has been in the past and what it will be like in the future if you do not change. Then spend some time thinking and imagining what it would be like to be a different person, imagine if your mind was naturally confident, relaxed, strong, kind and peaceful all the time. Imagine how it would feel to always meet challenging situations with a positive attitude. Think about how your quality of life would improve if your mind was like this. Then try to come to a deep inner determination to gradually move your mind in this direction, think 'I am going to spend the rest of my life steadily and consistently developing my mind'. Try to meditate on this positive thought for as long as is comfortable.

When you have finished make a short dedication like 'through the power of these positive thoughts may all living beings find lasting happiness' and try to carry your positive thoughts in to the rest of the day.

Use this page to make some notes on what you found thought-provoking or useful in this chapter:

3

PREPARATION FOR CHANGE

After reading this chapter you should be able to:

Understand the importance of good preparation in training your mind

Identify some clear goals and objectives

Have an idea of what you can realistically expect of yourself

Examine your past in a new light and begin a healing process

Learning to cope with serious challenges in life needs thought, planning and good preparation to achieve lasting results. We need to take a practical long-term approach. If we were a mountaineer considering our next major climb we might begin planning and training months or years in advance. In all areas of human endeavor it seems the two major factors that determine success are ambition and good planning. Whether we are an athlete, a businessman, a politician, a writer, a doctor or whatever to achieve great results we need to be constantly well motivated and well organized.

To begin with we need to establish our goal. If we are a mountaineer then it is easy, we decide which mountain we wish to climb and if we manage to reach the summit we have been successful.

But learning to cope with the more mundane problems of everyday life like illness, unemployment and disability by transforming and training our mind is much more subtle. What is our goal and how can we gauge our progress? Our goal is personal to us and might be different for others in a similar situation.

For some people who are experiencing severe illness their goal might be a complete physical cure, anything less than this might seem like failure. But what is the meaning of physical healing if our mind does not change? What is the purpose of life if we get everything we want? When children are brought up in an environment where all their wishes are granted they often become selfish, immature and impatient adults. Many people who have achieved their external ambitions of fame and wealth are often very unhappy. *When we constantly seek to fulfill our desires they just become stronger.* But if we learn how to be content whatever life throws at us our mind becomes strong and peaceful, our previously insatiable desires subside and we experience genuine happiness from within which does not depend on money or relationships or the weather! Ironically when we have a mind that does not need the temporary happiness that the external world offers we can enjoy our relationships and possessions much more because we are not so attached to them.

Contentment and inner peace bring freedom and flexibility to the mind. All our relationships become more meaningful; we become a better friend, partner, daughter etc. Because we are naturally happy from within we are less demanding or dependent upon others, we have much more to give and can be a real source of peace and support to others. Although we can use the difficulties we experience to help us develop special inner qualities suffering itself has no meaning. Suffering only becomes useful when we have the wisdom to use it to transform and expand our mind. Therefore the meaning of life is not to achieve temporary happiness through accumulating wealth or achieving fame neither is the meaning of life to suffer;

THE MEANING OF LIFE IS TO GROW

It is so important to understand this. This is our general goal; we can even take this as our mission statement for life. Without establishing a clear purpose in life it is easy to drift along through the various stages of life without ever really achieving anything worthwhile on the inside. At least if we have a definite goal we can make some progress in the direction that we think is best, then at the end of our life we can look back and be satisfied that we have done something we feel good about.

If we choose something like 'the meaning of my life is to grow' as a mission statement it can be very helpful to write it down in large letters, like a banner, and put it where you will see it every day, like the back of your bedroom door. Every morning take a look at it and think about your general goal in life and that will influence your day in a very positive way. It will help you to develop familiarity with a new perspective. It will remind you to see all 'problems' as opportunities to transform and develop your spiritual potential. *Whenever you have to make a serious choice in life just ask yourself, 'will this help me to grow, will this help me to become a better person?'*

Once we have a mission statement that we are happy with we can think about our specific goal or goals both in the short and long term. Again we need to choose something that we believe in, something that we think is attainable. It doesn't need to be our final goal it can just be our first step. For some people it might be letting go of anger about a difficult situation in the past or present, for others it might be accepting and living happily with a difficult illness, for some one else it might be a wish to become more confident and caring. The more specific we make our goals the more easily we can work out a practical plan to attain them. For example on a typical day how often do you feel a deep sense of inner peace, wellbeing or fulfillment, 20% of the time, 10%, Never? How often do you get angry during a typical week, five times, ten times, 100? In this way we can judge where we are at present, without being hard on ourselves or feeling guilty. We can identify where we want to be in one month or three months or one year or ten years. We can also use this method to gauge our progress, especially if we keep a diary of our successes and failures. Find a blank diary or notebook and start planning now, don't just let this be a good idea that you forget about in a few days.

Our goals for personal or spiritual development are really something only we can decide but there are some common to all religions and paths to personal growth like increased wisdom and compassion, less selfishness, more contentment, patience, empathy, inner peace, spiritual maturity, and a sense of closeness to God or Buddha or whatever we feel is out there or within us. You could develop your own code of conduct for life, a list of do's and don'ts, that give you some clear boundaries of behavior that can help you reach your inner goals.

We definitely need to take plenty of time to look at ourselves honestly and ask 'to what extent have I developed good inner qualities over the course of my life?' When we think about this regularly we will definitely begin to develop a deep wish to use the rest of our life in a meaningful way. If we do not develop this wish again and again sooner or later we will lose interest in our good plans and our deep-rooted familiarity to our previous approach to life will draw us back to our old ways.

It is helpful to know at the start of our training that our mind simply works on familiarity and because of this we can be easily influenced by others. This is how the mind of a child is shaped by their surroundings when they are young. If we are brought up in a hard environment without love or encouragement it is easy to develop a poor self image and through years of familiarity with this belief it becomes our own personal reality. We grow in to an adult with little confidence and it can feel that this is the way we will be for life. It is not until there is a break in the clouds that we see a possibility for inner change. The momentum of our past can be very strong and this is why people often don't change as they become adults. *Our behavior patterns can be strong enough to last a life time if we don't develop a strong and continuous wish to change for the better.*

However it is because our mind is a creature of habit that we can change and reshape our inner world into something special. Put very simply if we wake up one day and we decide that just for this day we are going to be kind, positive, loving, patient and happy then that day will definitely be special. Then if as a result of this good experience we decide again to act the same way the next day that day will also be special or at least a little better than our ordinary way of living. If we do this for a few weeks we will start to make an impact on the deeper levels of our mind and if we carry on for months or a few years we will create deep positive habits that will last a lifetime and longer. Our life can become all that we want it to be just through the power of our own effort to change within. It doesn't matter if our career is unsuccessful, our relationships fail or we have little money. With our mind empowered with positive energy even if the external world lets us down we will have a very positive and fulfilling life and become a good influence on others.

At some point we have to start to take control of our mind and again this begins with a wish to change based on the understanding that an uncontrolled mind is the source of all our problems. It is because we have little control over our mind that we become unhappy at the smallest thing. It doesn't take much to make us feel irritated, depressed or worried. Just a few misguided words from a friend can play on our mind and cause us to feel irritated all day. Every time we allow negative states of mind to arise and stay with us this is like self-harm. If we regularly hurt our own body by cutting our skin we would think this is serious and a sign of some deep mental or emotional problem. Yet we hurt our self every day by becoming negative or unhappy. *In the same way that we learned to control our body when we were a baby we can now learn to control our mind, it is when our mind is out of control that we get easily hurt and we easily hurt others.* We do not hurt our body because we do not want to experience pain and we can learn not to hurt our mind by remaining peaceful and positive and not allowing unhappy thoughts or feelings to take control of our life.

It is important to understand that we are not talking about suppressing negative states of mind since this would be as damaging as encouraging them. We are just learning to let them go as soon as possible and eventually, again just through the power of familiarity, they will stop appearing in our mind all together. Also this doesn't mean that we stop discriminating between right and wrong or allow other people to use us as a doormat by always being patient and helpful. Sometimes the kindest thing might be to stop others' negative behavior with strong words or actions and if our genuine motive is to help then we are within the boundaries of good behavior.

Sometimes we might think that a controlled mind is a tight or rigid mind and that happiness means the freedom to let our thoughts and emotions arise in whatever way they wish. Ironically the most natural and profound sense of freedom comes from having complete control over our mind. If we want a stable and lasting experience of inner peace we have to learn how to develop a stable and balanced mind. If all our problems are just negative states of mind then to gain freedom from unhappiness we have to develop the ability to avoid it by learning to control our mind. *Eventually we will be able to develop and keep a peaceful and positive state of mind all the time, whatever our external world is like. This is real freedom.*

This is easier said than done especially if we are suffering severe problems like a long-term illness, but at some point we have to acknowledge that if we want to at least gain a little quality of life this is the only way forward. Going back to the mountain analogy having a difficult problem to deal with is like suddenly finding our self at the foot of a huge mountain with no previous experience of mountaineering. It is much easier to start with small challenges and work our way up to the big ones, but sometimes we have no choice when we find ourselves facing an unavoidable illness, bereavement, accident or broken relationship. These things can seem far too big for us to consider transforming them into opportunities for spiritual growth. Just thinking about the size of the challenge ahead saps all our energy and will to be positive. So we have to be very practical and realistic, just set manageable targets, maybe just for one day every week we can try very hard to be relaxed and positive. Then for the rest of the week we can go back to feeling as we wish. Even small progress can make us feel empowered and see the future in a more positive light. It is much more likely that we will make sustained effort if we adopt this kind of relaxed long-term approach rather than putting all our energy into the first few weeks then becoming overwhelmed with disappointment when we become very upset over a small problem.

When we start a long journey we need to prepare well. We need to look into the future and try to think what our goals are and how we can achieve them and what preparations we need to make to increase our chance of success. Our journey is an inner journey but there are still things we need to take with us and things we need to leave behind. One of the things we need to leave behind is the past; it is difficult to begin a new life while we still have one foot in the past. Our past experiences can be like heavy weights in the mind. A mountaineer would never dream of taking unnecessary weight on an expedition because he knows how tiring it can be. Letting go of the past on a deep level can release lots of new energy that we need to progress along our inner journey.

We don't have to make physical changes in our life to let go of the past although sometimes this can be helpful. A change of address, new relationships, new career, new clothes etc can encourage and support an inner change to some degree. But these things can also be deceptive and have a short-lived effect on our quality of life if we are not really changing inside. Letting go of the past is mainly a mental and emotional release which we can achieve through clear thinking and the power of intention.

Firstly we have to acknowledge that the past is gone. We can never return, what is done is done. We cannot find the past, if we go to the places where we have had strong good or bad experiences those events are not still happening, it is over, gone. In fact everything has changed, on the surface it might seem that the physical environment is still there but in reality even a building or landscape changes completely moment by moment. In reality nothing exists for more than a moment everything is in the nature of change, everything is impermanent. It takes much contemplation and meditation to realize this on a deep level but just understanding this on a superficial level can still have quite an impact on our life in a very practical way. If we are aware that our friends and family, our career, our body, our life and everything around us are not solid and unchanging we will be released from reliance and expectation.

We rely on so many things outside our mind to be happy yet these things will change and disappear one day because their nature or essence is impermanence. We expect so much from life, from the future, but because everything is impermanent nothing is guaranteed in the material world. Thinking about this we have to come to the conclusion that the only way to cope with this truth is to let go. *If we can mentally release the past and have no expectations for the future we will find great peace in our mind.*

The only way the past exists is as a memory and memories are just pictures and feelings in the mind, as intangible as dreams. If we accept this it can help us to take past events less seriously and move on. Often we cannot move forward in life or in our personal growth because we keep reliving the past or we feel our current personality is shaped by our past. The latter is partly true but we believe this too much. We sometimes feel we are what our parents and life have made us and we can be no different. Obviously our parents have a big influence on us but if it was really down to our parents then all brothers and sisters would have the same personality. We are what we have made ourselves to be by reacting to life's experiences in a positive or negative way. Some children have the inner power to shrug off a difficult childhood and live a very positive life; from a Buddhist view this is because they have some familiarity with accepting difficulties and developing their mind from a previous life.

Once we realize that we have the power to react as we wish this can release us from a negative outlook or a repetitive pattern of thought or feeling. Training our mind to look at the past in this way can be a very practical way to begin to accept, heal, let go and move on. But sometimes we have to also accept that this is a process that can take time. In one sense there is no rush, we need to do things steadily and genuinely, but in another sense there is no time to waste!

Many people become depressed and burdened with the mental weight of coping with long-term problems. We have all experienced the boredom and frustration of having a bad cold or flu but try to imagine having difficult symptoms for months or years like people with MS or cancer. Imagine the grinding and constant pain endured with arthritis or serious back or joint problems, yet so many people are facing these difficulties daily. Expanding our mind and understanding that we are not alone with suffering can make us feel more peaceful. Also empathy and understanding towards the suffering of others can induce a sense of inner peace because we are less focused on our own problems. In this way illness or any difficult problem can become a useful tool for personal growth instead of just an experience of suffering. But the first step is learning to let go of the past and accept the present then we can start to steadily build a stable, meaningful and beautiful future.

As mentioned, one of the main points to consider as part of this process is that whatever we have been through has passed it is not all with us today. Today is what we have to work with so feeling bitter or depressed about what has happened in the past will leave us little power or energy to mentally transform the present, meaning our future will be the same as the past. ***Decide to make a fresh start every day and take this day as the most important day in our life.***

We definitely need to start to consider becoming a different person by transforming our outlook and approach to life. We are impermanent; our inner world is as changeable as our external world. You are not the same person now as you were ten or twenty years ago. We know people can change in a very short time. Life-changing events like new relationships, bereavement, crime, marriage, children and serious illness can change someone for better or worse on the inside. So we know we can change, what we don't know is we can change just through the power of our own wish and daily effort without external forces pushing us one way or another. Just knowing that we can change through our own will can bring a whole new energy and enthusiasm to our life, now we have something to look forward to.

There are different ways we can learn to accept a problem. One is to simply understand that not accepting it will not cure it or make us feel better in any way. On the other hand accepting our situation, and this does not mean 'giving in', will definitely make us feel better and might even help the healing process. ***Accepting a difficult situation as a positive challenge can really empower us and help us to focus on dealing constructively with the task in hand.***

Making a firm decision to put all our energy into solving a problem takes energy away from worrying about it. In this sense we need to be warrior like, gather all our energy and project our mind in a positive direction every day. Maybe we can do this every day for the rest of our life, why not? What a life that would be. We also need the wisdom to use this enthusiasm and energy in a useful way. There is no point in thinking 'I am going to get well', 'I am going to get well' if this is not likely to happen. We need to focus our energy on achieving wise and manageable goals that will improve our quality of life principally through transforming our mental and emotional outlook.

One aspect of acceptance is to stop seeing difficult people, illness or any 'problem' as the enemy and to start seeing negative states of mind like worry, depression and anger as the real enemy. Again this is not 'giving in', of course we need to take all the practical steps necessary to help our body heal. In fact what we are doing by correctly identifying the enemy is facing up to problems and taking our power back. We stop letting the problem control our quality of life and we can actually start to use our difficult situation to improve our quality of life. Previously the stressful situation was feeding and supporting the enemy but now just through the power of our wisdom we are using that same problem to destroy the enemy of an unhappy mind. *Sometimes it is helpful to think over and over 'my main problem is just an unhappy mind'.*

Some people might be inspired to change completely overnight, this does happen. But generally a steady long-term approach is more realistic. What we want to be able to do is look back in a few months time and feel some permanent inner change, not total change but just feeling something small has changed forever. If we carry on in this way our life will be something good for the world. A big inner shift for only a short time often has no lasting impact and can leave us feeling like a failure when we lose our enthusiasm. We need to be an enthusiastic realist then our dreams and wishes will steadily become our reality and one day we will look back and feel our life has been really worthwhile.

As mentioned, another way to accept the past and a difficult present situation is to understand the laws of Karma. This natural universal law explains why we sometimes experience good things and sometimes bad things in our life. It also explains how we can shape our own future rather than being a slave to the karmic lottery of ordinary life. We do not have to be Buddhist to benefit from such ideas, understanding karma and living accordingly is also just a very practical and logical way to improve our life.

Forgiveness is very important to be able to move on. If we cannot forgive we will be trapped in the past and our will and energy to change will be weak. Letting go of anger and hurt is so healing, brave and wise. When someone hurts us or we experience some serious misfortune this is one problem but we often add to this by developing negative states of mind like anger, depression, stress, fear, etc. These make a difficult situation much worse so we need to learn to respond to such situations in a positive way and this will make our life much smoother and enjoyable.

Many people would say that fear and depression and similar mindsets are just a natural human response to major problems. This is true for most of us at present but it is not true for all of us. Some people respond to problems in a very positive way and we can definitely learn to do the same. If we regard our self as a spiritual child at the start of our inner journey, if we understand that we are right at the beginning, we will not expect too much of our self in the same way that a loving parent does not expect too much of there child but has great hope for their future. A loving parent might want their child to grow up to be honest, hard working, kind, responsible, wise and warm hearted but they know that it takes time and many mistakes to get there. They naturally take a healthy long-term approach and work hard on a daily basis to achieve their long-term goal. What keeps them going is an understanding that the long-term goal is very worthwhile. If we have a similar approach it is definite that we can achieve our goals of personal transformation and help others achieve similar results.

Another way of letting go of the past is to look to the future. If we are always going over what has happened in our life or we suppress negative emotions about the past we cannot begin to create a healthier world. It is an amazing truth that the whole process of dealing with illness can make us feel more alive than ever before. Illness and other challenges can turn our life around, particularly when our own mortality becomes part of the equation. Initially this can be a very unpleasant experience but once we start to look for opportunities to learn and transform through adversity we might start to feel like we are on the verge of a wonderful voyage of discovery initiated by our own illness. Some people even view death as a great adventure, a voyage into the beyond, and many spiritual practitioners actually look forward to death as they feel it is an opportunity to return to God. What an amazing and life-affirming attitude. Whatever mountain we are faced with in life we have to put ourselves in charge, the moment we allow negative thoughts and feelings to take control we have lost the day. Talk to any athlete, business executive or serious spiritual practitioner and they will tell you that whatever your goal, success can only be realized if you are in the driving seat mentally and emotionally.

Sometimes it is necessary to talk to yourself and pull yourself together, even tell yourself off if it works! Although gentle self-encouragement is sometimes better especially if you are feeling a little fragile. Find out through your own experience what works for you in different situations and put your newfound self-knowledge into practice. *Do whatever you need to do to motivate yourself, if you give up, nothing will change.*

Long-term illness or a series of difficult life experiences can leave us mentally and emotionally beaten and wondering 'What is the meaning of life? What can I do with my life now?' Our ordinary world can be shattered by difficult experiences and this can be terrible but perhaps necessary for a genuine change or inner revelation to take place. When we are put in a difficult situation that is beyond our normal control or capacity we are forced to reach out for help from a higher source or we are forced to discover some profound inner strength or understanding or acceptance or sense of letting go in order to survive. When we have experienced something like this beyond our normal life, who would want to return? We need to stay young, to keep a sense of wonder and to keep searching and questioning otherwise our life becomes spiritually poor, we will not evolve and will leave this world with nothing special to show for our time here.

Adversity can really open our mind to the wonders of the universe and the wonders of our own inner potential where we can find the answers to all our problems and experience infinite clarity, love and power to transform and heal our own life and the lives of others. I have to say this again, illness and any challenging situation can be a real blessing in disguise. If we have this positive approach we can look toward a future of hope and wonder, discovery and transformation. Even if we only have a short time to live that time can be very special, like the beginning of a new life, a new way of living. At the time of our death this new attitude can send us in the right direction for continuing our spiritual growth in the future.

What kind of future do we want to create? As mentioned, the past is just pictures and feelings in the mind, but the future is even less tangible than this. For most people the future is just an extension of the present but when we start to move into the world of personal transformation we are opening up doors to the possibility of dramatic change. Because the future has not happened yet we can shape it, our future is in our hands. Many people apply this understanding in the ordinary world and achieve amazing results. People in all walks of life achieve many amazing things just by having the attitude that a successful future can be created through the power of positive thought and action.

If we are affected by a serious problem we can feel that the world has left us behind. Perhaps at one time we had dreams that have been shattered by our physical limitations and our future seems bleak. But perhaps this is not the case, perhaps we are at an advantage. If we develop our wisdom a little we may start to perceive an inner potential that is a much greater and more profound achievement than could ever be achieved in the way that people normally live their lives.

Think about the great spiritual teachers who have touched the world in a very positive way. People like Jesus, Buddha, Mohammed, Krishna, Ghandi and many others, they all had special minds with great inner horizons. They looked beyond the limitations of the material world, developed their inner world and touched the lives of millions. Because we are so familiar with our external world we think that the best way to help others is in practical, material ways. When others are in need we try to help relieve their suffering by providing whatever they require, like food, shelter, clothes etc. Of course this kind of help is essential, we all need to have the basics to survive and there is no reason why we shouldn't have a very comfortable material life as well. But the best thing we can give to others is the ability to solve their own problems forever. First we need to experience this truth for our self and illness or other challenges can be a gateway to this special achievement. Misfortune can cause us much suffering or it can cause us to aspire to some new remarkable goals that we would never have previously considered. Perhaps our body is limited by illness but our mind is free. *Perhaps we cannot do what we wanted to do in life, but what can we achieve by developing our mind?* We don't know yet because we are right at the start of our journey but we need to consider this well because it will give us much energy to proceed and help let go of anger and frustration about our difficult situation.

In Buddhism and other eastern traditions the culmination of the inner journey is enlightenment, in Christianity it is a closeness or unity with God, in terms of personal growth it is about becoming a more whole, healthy and complete human being. There is such similarity amongst these different ideologies although they were developed separately, suggesting that the spiritual or inner journey is the real meaning of a human life. Just getting to the point where we are considering starting this journey is quite an achievement when the tide of the world is pulling in the opposite direction. So we should feel quite pleased with our progress and prepare for an even brighter future. *Because of, rather than in spite of, adversity, in our own small way, day by day, we can become a spiritual light for the world.*

The essential points from this chapter are:

You need to have a mission statement before you begin and then develop some specific and realistic goals and maybe a code of conduct. Much of our energy or life force is blocked or locked in the past, we need to be courageous enough to revisit major events and trauma, compassionate enough to forgive ourselves or others and wise enough to let go and move on. We can't become a better person while we are still living in the past. We need the challenges and difficulties in life to grow. We are deeply spiritual beings and without a spiritual aspect to our life we are not fully alive.

Exercise:

Visit some places you have not been to for a long time. Maybe the place where you grew up or if you cannot physically be there spend some time clearly remembering. It might help to write down some of your most powerful memories. Try to clearly identify positive aspects of your personality that have come from these life experiences, even if they were traumatic. If you feel strong negative emotions arising don't allow yourself to be swamped by them and don't suppress them, just allow them to arise and dissipate like waves on an ocean. Search within yourself for some meaning to these experiences, this can help to put the past in context and allow you to be more alive now.

Now try a meditation:

When your mind has settled down develop a good intention like 'may every living being benefit from this meditation'. Spend a few minutes doing the gentle breathing meditation explained in chapter 4. Then meditate using the following contemplation:

Think about what it means to be a spiritual being. What would it mean to have a spiritual aspect to your life? From one point of view it simply means steadily striving to become a better person. Bring to mind your mission statement and the specific goals you have decided to aim towards and try to come to a deep conviction that this is one of the most important aspects of your life and focus you mind on this decision. This is your object of meditation, try to hold it for as long as possible.

When you have finished make a short dedication like 'through the power of these positives thoughts may all living beings find lasting happiness' and try to carry your positive thoughts into the rest of the day.

Use this page to make some notes on what you found thought-provoking or useful in this chapter:

4

PRACTICAL MEDITATION

After reading this chapter you should be able to:

Understand the benefits of meditation

Know the basic techniques of meditation

Begin a daily meditation practice

There are many different types of meditation, most of them aim to relax the body and mind and promote peaceful and positive states of mind. Meditation is a very simple, natural and powerful way of realizing our ability to become more whole, healthy and happy human beings from within. Meditation is not difficult; we can receive great benefit even from our very first meditation session. The benefits of regular meditation are now well known. We gain improved health and wellbeing, levels of stress are greatly reduced and positive, peaceful and confident states of mind are easily generated.

The main function of meditation is to help us become familiar with a positive state of mind. At present we react to difficult circumstances often with a negative mind because that is what we are most familiar with. *We put our own happiness before others simply because we are so familiar with thinking and feeling that we are more important.* Meditation helps us to control our mind and learn to react to the challenges of life in a more positive way. Most of the problems we experience in life arise because our mind is uncontrolled. Negative thoughts and feelings like anger, jealousy, boredom, impatience, depression and loneliness arise because we have little control over our inner landscape, the weather changes very quickly inside our mind! At the moment our happiness or quality of life is very fragile because our mind is fragile. Externally we might be healthy and strong and 'successful' but internally we are weak and vulnerable. It doesn't take much to destroy our inner peace, just a few harsh words, a missed train, a little rain, a crying baby. Negative thoughts and feelings are very unpleasant to experience, they are a long way from a clear, balanced and happy mind. So if we had a choice who would want to experience them? Of course nobody wants to be unhappy, we all try to find happiness and avoid problems all the time, but this is a pointless quest unless we learn to control our mind.

Meditation is a very practical tool for accessing a reservoir of deep inner peace and contentment from within your own mind. It is a very relaxing and natural process and shouldn't be rushed and we shouldn't expect too much too soon. Just like learning to swim or drive or fly a plane we need to be consistent, methodical and enthusiastic and then good results are guaranteed. In this chapter we will just look at breathing meditation, which is mainly a preliminary to further meditation but still very powerful and helpful for developing inner peace. At the end of every other chapter in this book there is a contemplation and placement meditation, this is the main type of meditation we need to become familiar with if we want to change on a deep level. If you want to know more about this kind of meditation look at *The New Meditation Handbook* by Geshe Kelsang Gyatso (Tharpa Publications).

Our breath and our mind are closely linked, if we learn how to control our breathing this can help us to control our mind. When someone is anxious their breathing is very shallow and rapid, when someone is relaxed or asleep their breathing is deep and slow. In breathing meditation we concentrate our mind on the sensation of breathing, particularly the gentle sensation of the breath at the tip of the nose as the cool air comes in and the warm air goes out. Because this is a subtle physical sensation it is quite difficult to keep our mind focused on it as there may be stronger physical sensations, thoughts and sounds that our mind is easily distracted by.

All we have to do is to find the object of meditation, the gentle sensation of the breath in the nostrils, and keep our attention focused on this one thing. If our mind wanders off as soon as we notice this we mentally 'find' the object of meditation again and try to stay focused on it for as long as possible. As we progress in our practice we will be able to stay focused on the object of meditation for longer and longer and our meditation sessions will become more and more enjoyable and fruitful. Start by meditating for just ten minutes once or twice a day. It is better to have a short meditation session and really try to make it count than a long one with poor concentration.

To meditate well we also need a good posture and our body needs to be relaxed. The main thing is to keep our back fairly straight; this keeps our mind alert and allows our inner energies to flow freely. We can sit on a chair or on the floor but if we are confined to a bed we can meditate whilst lying down. If you have time you can start by relaxing your body, bring your attention to your toes and try to 'find' any tension and release it. At first it may be helpful to tense and then release them, we need to gradually familiarize ourselves with the experience of consciously relaxing, then the process will become easier.

Move your attention slowly into the rest of your feet consciously relaxing each part. If it helps you can think 'release and relax' as you slowly bring your attention to the ankles, shins, calves, knees etc. Continue to move your attention up through the body, relaxing each part. If your attention wanders, simply return to where you were up to. When you have reached the top of your head spend a few minutes being aware of how it feels to be completely relaxed. The more we remember this experience the easier it will become to repeat and carry forward into our daily activities. This technique can take some time to master so don't be disappointed if you still feel some tension after the first few sessions, this will pass in time and the technique will become natural. Then with your eyes gently closed, or slightly open if you are a little sleepy or tired, begin your breathing meditation.

Towards the end of your meditation if your mind has become peaceful and relaxed you can spend a few minutes using that feeling of inner peace as your object of meditation. Again try to keep your attention focused on it without being distracted by other feelings, thoughts or sounds. You can also use the last few minutes of meditation to concentrate on a specific positive thought or feeling that relates to the inner qualities you are trying to develop or some difficulty that you are trying to accept/transform.

At the end of your meditation session make a determination to keep hold of that feeling of inner peace all day. Obviously you will lose it sooner or later and when you do try to remember how you felt during meditation and bring that feeling back. Don't worry at all if you cannot do this, it does take a long time of patient inner training to be able to generate and hold a happy mind for long periods of time so again be realistic, relax and enjoy the challenge of creating a completely new inner landscape. You can meditate in this way all day and in all situations, all you need to do is be aware. Be aware of how you are feeling. If you are feeling negative just try to remember how you felt in meditation or if it is possible do a few minutes' breathing meditation again.

The essential points from this chapter are:
Meditation is a very simple technique that anyone can practice successfully. The more regular meditation you do the more peaceful and controlled your mind will become. When our mind is happy and relaxed we are happy and relaxed! In this way we can find the happiness that we are all looking for from within.

Exercise:
Set your self some meditation goals, like a determination to do some breathing meditation for may be ten minutes every day for one week. Then if you manage to keep to this, set your sights a little higher, do two ten-minute meditations every day for one week or one a day for two weeks. Eventually you will find it easy to find the time to meditate because you will notice that life is much more enjoyable when your mind is happy and relaxed!

Now try a meditation:
Try the breathing meditation explained in this chapter. Remember, don't worry if your mind becomes very busy the moment you try to concentrate on the gentle sensation of breathing, this happens to almost everyone at first, you are just becoming aware of how busy your mind really is. It might take a few days or even a few weeks before this settles down, don't expect too much too soon and you might be pleasantly surprised, almost everyone experiences at least one 'good' meditation in the first few days.

Use this page to make some notes on what you found thought-provoking or useful in this chapter:

5

TECHNIQUES FOR INNER CHANGE

After reading this chapter you should be able to:

Incorporate some useful ideas in to your plan for training your mind

Understand some of the potential pitfalls and how to avoid them

Understand that acceptance is the first step towards inner change

Begin to let go of negative habits

As mentioned we need to think about developing a strategy or plan of inner transformation. It can be really helpful to use a blank notepad or diary to make notes of the things you plan to do and to chart your progress. If we have some record of how we are progressing this can be really revealing and encouraging. We can choose a date to start this project - sometimes it is better to choose a date in the future perhaps in five or seven days time, this gives us some time to enjoy planning what we are going to do, discuss it with others and work out a realistic schedule that we think we can keep to.

Training our mind can be very similar to training our body. If we went to a gym and employed a personal trainer to transform us into a fit and strong person we would expect them to take some time developing a realistic regime of exercise and diet and to be professional and consistent in their approach. So in this instance we can be our own personal trainer and do the same with regard to our mind. We might simply decide that for the first week we will spend just a few minutes trying to concentrate on a positive thought at the start of every day. Write this in your diary and tick it every time you have completed the task. Then record anything special or positive that happens as a result of this new activity. At the end of the week sit down and work out what you want to do the following week; you may want to do the same again or you may want to try something extra. Everyone can spare just a few minutes at the start of the day so there is no excuse for not being able to find the time!

One of the advantages of putting your time and effort in to an inner project like this is that you are guaranteed results, it can never be a waste of time. Sometimes our external ambitions are thwarted by circumstances beyond our control, we often see people experiencing failure in business and sport and other ventures despite tremendous effort and commitment. On the other hand, whatever difficulties we experience as part of our inner training programme can become another rung on our ladder to success. Any problem or worry is an opportunity to grow. If we build this attitude in to our programme whatever difficulties we encounter can only lead to greater success.

If we have more time we can begin our mind-training programme by doing 10-15 minutes meditation at the start of each day. Just begin with the simple breathing meditation explained in the previous chapter and if you like, at the end of the meditation choose a positive thought for the day like 'I will always be kind to others' and try to remember this thought throughout the day.

If we are coming to terms with a difficult illness then maybe the first thing we need to do is to think, how can I begin to simply accept this difficult situation? *It is impossible to develop a happy and peaceful mind if we are full of fear, anger or depression.* Of course these emotions are natural in the first stages of illness and we shouldn't make things worse by being hard on ourselves and feeling like a failure if we cannot let go of them. But in our own time we have to accept that in reality these emotions serve no useful purpose and only make a difficult situation much worse. The sooner we can move our mind towards an inner experience of acceptance the better for us and those close to us. Acceptance doesn't mean that we can't try to improve our situation externally. If there are ways we can improve our health we should always take such steps, but if there is not much we can do externally there is always plenty we can do to improve our situation from within. It does take much courage and effort to begin with, especially when we are faced with a seemingly insurmountable challenge but if we just try a little each day to swim against the tide of anger or depression within us we will become gradually stronger and eventually overcome these negative emotions that destroy our inner peace and happiness. Simple logic dictates that this approach must be better than allowing our self to be carried away on the tide of disturbing and useless states of mind. The quicker we gain control over our inner world the brighter our future will be whatever our level of health or external comfort. This sense of optimism will give us more energy to further develop our mind and we will find our self on a partly self-sustaining upward spiral of spiritual and personal growth.

How can we practically begin to change from within? How do we transform a negative thought or emotion in to a positive one? How can we prevent negative thoughts and feelings from arising and keep a happy and peaceful mind all the time?

Simply repeating a positive affirmation or spending a few minutes in meditation at the start of the day can set our mind in the right direction and then one thing follows on from another and we are more likely to have a day of positive feelings and experiences. Throughout the day we can keep one eye on what our mind is doing every now and then without being too obsessive, and check to see if we are still feeling positive and relaxed. This regular checking process is the key to transforming our mind, it strengthens our mind so that we can build the ability within to keep a positive attitude for longer and longer periods of time.

When you check your mind and notice that you are feeling a bit sad, lonely or irritated try to let go of this and develop a positive thought which will lead to a positive emotion and then again try to keep this feeling while you are going about your daily activities. One method to let go of negative feelings is to simply remember that the negative emotion is completely useless and it is actually harming you like a thorn in your foot, from this logical reasoning the desire to let go will eventually arise in your mind. Then the next step is simply to repeat a positive thought to yourself like 'may everyone be happy' or 'all I need is a happy mind' or 'let go and relax' or anything else that is powerful for you.

At first when you try these techniques you might feel that nothing is happening and that they don't work or it may feel artificial like you are just pretending to be positive when really you don't feel positive. But don't worry about this, we are just starting this journey so we won't get to our destination in just one day, we are just taking the first steps in the right direction. When we start to actually want our mind to be positive, happy and relaxed this in itself is quite an achievement.

Most people do not blame their problems on their own mind! So if we start to feel that the problem is inside rather than outside this is a sign we are developing some wisdom. If we really want something there is a good chance we are going to put in enough effort required to achieve it.

When you develop a positive thought with the wish to improve your mind this is a wonderful thing. Not many people in the world are doing this, you should feel some sense of being a pioneer. *The new frontier of human development is not outer space but the wonders of inner space.* Someone who has a serious illness and maybe even confined to a bed or wheelchair may be at the forefront of human evolution. External development including space travel will never bring what human beings really wish for. The history of humanity is characterized by the search for happiness and freedom from suffering so again the meaning of life for a human is simply to find genuine lasting happiness and this can only come from inner or spiritual development. If lasting happiness could be attained through external development someone would have done it by now! Yet many people have achieved the ultimate happiness of spiritual enlightenment through inner development. Perhaps we don't seem to meet them very often but that might be because we have never really looked for them or valued that way of life. Profound spiritual achievements come through inner development. Of course external development is necessary, we all deserve a good standard of living, but beyond this external development only brings temporary happiness. Material or external success can take us away from grasping the essence of our life before it is over.

Sometimes mind-training techniques can seem too simple to be effective. But in many ways the mind is quite a simple machine, as mentioned it simply works on familiarity. Training the mind is just a matter of developing good inner habits. At first it feels unnatural because feeling light and positive most of the time is not our natural habit. But our personality is not physical, it is not fixed, we know from our own experience that over the course of our life it changes naturally. So all we are doing here is taking advantage of our own impermanence by taking control of the naturally changing inner landscape of the mind and creating something special.

When we get discouraged it can be very helpful to remember that our job is to create something special. Transforming our mind or personality is a creative process, but it has much more meaning and benefit for the world than any work of art or scientific discovery. If we are suffering from a long-term illness we should never feel that we are a useless member of society, in fact if we develop our mind we can become one of the most important or valuable people in the world. Just remember all living beings want to find lasting happiness, happiness is just a state of mind, it comes from within. *If we can develop a stable experience of natural happiness from within we have found what the world is looking for!* How special and profound is that? We can share this way of living with others by talking about it at appropriate times when others are ready to listen or simply by being a living example of some one who has found what we all want. When others see that we are happy and relaxed even while we are ill or in a difficult situation they will gradually learn from our good example that all we need is a peaceful and happy mind.

The only way we can solve all the problems of the world is if people learn to be peaceful, content and happy and sincerely care for each other. If different cultures, religions and countries cared for each other there would be no famine, war or environmental problems in the world. Most of the problems of the world could be solved within a few years. If we carry on caring more about external development and our own happiness this world will continue to degenerate and eventually self-destruct.

Many people in the so-called developed world end up in a life of crime or drugs or depression. This downward spiral can start simply with a little discontentment in the mind and end in self-destruction through suicide or overdose or murder. This is the extreme example of what happens if we do not try to develop a controlled, peaceful and happy mind. Lack of self-control and discontentment causes many families to self-destruct. Lack of patience and care for each other causes our relationships to degenerate and people who once wanted to be together forever end up hating each other. All these difficult situations that are unfolding all over the world as you read this arise simply because our minds are out of our own control. If we develop a controlled, peaceful, caring and happy mind there would be no basis for big problems to arise and throw our life in to chaos. Whatever difficulties arose for us we would react in a positive and balanced way and actually grow through wisely experiencing challenging life situations. When looked at like this there is no choice! We have to grasp this opportunity to change the outer world by changing our inner world.

When you try to develop your mind you might feel like your mind won't listen to you! Of course we all want to feel relaxed and happy and confident but it is easier said than done. Sometimes our mind can feel like a spoilt child that just wants to do its own thing and not go in the direction we want it to. May be we wake up one day and we feel sad and lonely, obviously we don't want to feel like that but sometimes such feelings can be difficult to drop or replace with positive ones. The worst thing we can do is to get frustrated, we need to give ourselves time to change and realistically it takes months and years to change on a deep level. But if we don't begin this journey at some time in our life we will never evolve or progress. ***Our mind is like a garden, if it is not carefully tended it becomes wild and over grown.***

Some days we have to be firm with our mind and sometimes we have to be gentle and encouraging, a little like training a puppy or bringing up a child! We can be firm by remembering that if we don't train our mind it will degenerate like a wild garden or we can remember that we are adding to the problems of the world by living in a selfish way. If we believe in the laws of Karma we can also remember that living a selfish life only leads to suffering in future lives. On days when we feel we need to be more gentle and encouraging rather than firm we can think that what we are doing by training our mind is helping to make the world a better place, we are becoming a more mature, whole and complete human being, we are a pioneer because not many people in the world are trying to develop their inner qualities.

Even if we wake up one day and our mind is feeling too heavy or negative to change we can still think 'even though I don't feel good today may I learn to develop a happy and peaceful mind in the future'. Just repeating this thought while we are in the shower or getting dressed is a little victory, we have not surrendered to our mind, we are trying to develop it or develop the wish to change, which is vital if we want positive results in the future. Quite often gently repeating positive wishes, especially at the start of the day, can cause our mind to turn around and we begin to feel light and more positive. This kind of mind training is especially useful if we have a busy life. Although we may be busy if we think about it we can usually find many opportunities to develop our positive wishes. There are many activities that we do during the day where we can think about something else as well, for example eating, driving, getting washed and dressed, in the shower or bath, on the bus, waiting in a queue, shopping, walking, lying in bed and probably many other times.

Obviously your concentration won't be as good as during quiet meditation but you will be surprised how powerful these mini meditations can be. Also many people find formal meditation quite difficult to begin with so this kind of gentle mind training can be a great introduction and support to our developing meditation practice. Often this kind of training is said to be of more importance than formal meditation sessions principally because formal meditation might only last for twenty minutes but we can spend many hours developing our mind in normal everyday situations. However, periods of quiet contemplation, prayer and formal meditation are really important because we need periods of deep inner peace to experience the spiritual essence of our mind, which is the foundation of mind training. Without this we are only scratching the surface of our mind.

Connecting our mind training to regular daily activities keeps our practice regular and sustained. Often we can get very enthusiastic at the beginning of our new way of life but then completely forget about it after a few weeks! If we just choose one type of positive thought and relate it to a regular daily activity this can help us get into a very positive habit, then after a few weeks we will find ourselves naturally starting to think or feel positive as soon as we begin that activity. For example, every time we have a shower gently think a positive thought like 'may everyone be happy', or 'may I learn to develop a positive and peaceful mind' or 'may I become a more confident and relaxed person' or anything else we feel comfortable with. Just keep slowly repeating this kind of thought while you are showering and see how you feel when you are finished! If you do this for a few weeks you will find yourself naturally developing a positive thought every time you step in to the shower! This process of transforming or training our mind can be even more powerful if we can relate our thought to the chosen activity, when we are showering we can think 'may I develop a clear and peaceful mind' or 'may I clean away the negativity from my mind' or 'I am letting go of the past', try to actually feel your negative thoughts, past problems or trauma are being washed away. If you are driving think 'may I drive my life in a positive direction', if you are waiting for a bus 'may I learn to be patient and relaxed when the things I want don't come straight away', if you are cleaning the house 'I am cleaning the negative thought patterns from my mind'. Again we have to make it very personal and be creative and put some time and energy in to thinking how best this technique can work for us. Make a list of all the situations in your life where you can use this technique, then choose one for the first week, two for the second week and so on, until you have built up a sustainable schedule without taking on too much. We can be creative and vary our positive thoughts from time to time whilst still keeping them concentrated on the same main theme, this keeps them fresh and alive and they continue to have an impact on our mind. As soon as an affirmation loses its power to make you feel better try to change it slightly or think of a completely new one or sometimes all you need to do is think a little deeper why this affirmation is important to you and it will regain its power to help.

Don't underestimate how powerful this technique can be. *Gently and consistently repeating a positive thought will definitely have a profound impact on our personality and outlook.* Especially if this is combined with a programme of other activities like meditation, prayer, counseling, homeopathy, bach flower remedies, shiatsu, reiki or anything else you think might help your progression. There are so many opportunities nowadays for help and support with personal and spiritual growth, it can be a real revelation and joy to spend a year exploring the options that are available and finding the right combination that works for us. However there is also much to be said for choosing one complete spiritual path or way of life and making that your main focus, this way spiritual progress can be more clear and direct, see appendix 1.

Some spiritual practitioners who are trying to train in compassion use phrases like 'may I learn to cherish others more than myself' or 'may I learn to care for all living beings' or 'may everyone be happy'. Thoughts like these are very 'mind expanding' and especially powerful for solving our daily problems as they move our mind away from our own situation and help us to focus more on the happiness of others. If we care for someone who is far away we may often find ourselves thinking about them even though we do not see them very often. It is possible to start to feel this way toward all living beings, even though we have never met them in this life. If we regularly pray for the welfare of our world this will naturally bring peace to our mind because to genuinely care for so many others is a very powerful positive thought and helps us to let go of self obsession and look beyond our own small world.

If we can do all this skillfully without falling into the extremes of over enthusiasm or laziness in time we will become a very happy person with a deep sense of love and compassion for others. *When we think less about our own desires our mind naturally become more content and peaceful. The best way to do this is to simply focus more on others.* Again it does take time to change on a deep level and old habits die hard so we have to be very patient, persistent and skillful.

But using this gentle technique of coaxing our mind out of self obsession toward caring for others by repeating positive thoughts can give us a good experience of inner change quite quickly which will encourage us to keep practicing for a long time.

Eventually if we progress at our own manageable and natural pace we will find that our whole life can become a meditation for positive living. If we can combine this with a regular daily time for formal meditation we will have a wonderful life, guaranteed! In this way we can free ourselves from much of the discontent and suffering that most humans experience as they go through life. In a small way we become a liberated being because our happiness stops coming from unreliable sources and starts coming from within. This experience, however small, should be really valued as a sign that our life is definitely going in the right direction. Think how much suffering humans experience because of relationship problems. Since the beginning of time humans have always experienced many problems with poor relationships, all violence, wars and human rights violations come from relationship problems. But if we can learn to be happy with our self and content with who we are and what we have we do not need to control, dominate or rely on others. By becoming a happier person we become a better person and we are more useful to our friends and family. By training our mind and accessing that deep well of natural inner peace within us we can become a tower of strength for others.

Again it is very important not to be too zealous or tight with mind-training techniques, we need to have a very easy, light and relaxed attitude. If we push too hard our mind will often try to go in the opposite direction and we will lose heart easily. If we project too much energy at a problem it can just become bigger because we are taking it too seriously. By starting our training just with regular gentle positive thoughts we learn from our own experience that the mind is a delicate thing and although we do need to be firm and disciplined we also need to be skillful and gradually entice or seduce our mind in the right direction!

Every time you feel bored or feel like giving in you can do one of two things, take a break or push through. Again you will have to learn through experience which course of action is appropriate, if you take the wrong option you will take a step backward but if you sit down and take some time to work out why you did that and how you can learn to recognize which is the best option you have transformed a failure in to a success. *The whole process is about being honest with ourselves and beginning to recognize our motivation.* Often we will think now is the right time to ease off because that selfish part of our mind that does not want us to change is causing us to feel bored or tired. Sometimes that same part of our mind also gets over enthusiastic and makes us feel we are indestructible and now is the time to push ourselves to the limit when in fact we need to take a break. So keep one eye on your mind and check yourself before you act, but don't be afraid to make lots of mistakes!

Sharing your experiences with a friend or seeking some kind of professional help from a good counselor or therapist can be very helpful. If you have ever had counseling you will know that when someone is with you and listening to you without judgment but just letting you open up and freely explore your problems it acts as a catalyst for gaining deeper insights in to your own mind and helps you to establish clearly where you are in your personal growth. *A good listener is like a clear mirror helping us to see ourselves without trying to distort the truth.* One of the best things we can do for others is to become a good listener. Sometimes our friends may not feel comfortable with our deep feelings or simply because they love us and don't like to see us in emotional turmoil they say things to keep us away from going to those places within that we need to experience, understand, release and heal. If we don't go to those places we cannot heal them and they stay within us and hold us back from deep inner change.

If we do not know someone who is a good listener it can be very helpful to find a quiet place and take some time to just write down a list of the things that are on our mind. This list can be very extensive, if we feel there are many events from our past that need healing just write a list of them all and maybe even take a few weeks to gradually work through them. Take each event in turn and examine it under four headings. The first is 'what happened'. Take yourself back in time and write down clearly what actually happened without apportioning blame or allowing strong feelings to overwhelm you. Check over what you have written and make sure all the details are correct and nothing is foggy or hazy in your mind. Then the next section is 'how I felt'. Again allow yourself to go back to the event and remember how you felt, allow yourself to feel any strong emotions and write them down. The next section on your sheet of paper is 'how I feel now'. Again let the feelings come through and write them down. The next section is the most important and needs the most attention, this section we can call something like 'what next?' or 'the way forward' or 'how I would like to feel', choose something that rings true for you. The purpose of this section is to establish how a compassionate, wise and mature person would deal with this situation. Use your imagination, how would a spiritual or holy person deal with this? Obviously we may not be able to do this but using this method helps us to see beyond how we would normally try to solve our problems and gives us an idea where we can be in the future. Finally in the same section we write a conclusion, a course of realistic action that might not be the most altruistic but stretches us a little beyond our normal way of dealing with problems. Then we strongly decide that is what we will do! This is a great way of dealing with current problems as well as past events without getting bogged down in negative emotions or hiding from them.

If we can't imagine what being a better person might be like it is difficult to move forward in our training because our direction is not clear. In the same way as we dream about becoming an astronaut or train driver when we are a child we need to dream about becoming a better person, happy, relaxed, caring, patient, enthusiastic, committed, mature, playful, flexible, strong, confident, humble, compassionate and wise. We can have our head in the clouds and dream about these ideals as long as we have our feet on the ground and deal in realistic goals and little victories. Again, writing down the qualities that we would like to develop can be very helpful.

Another useful mind-training method is to write a list of the situations, challenges or difficulties in everyday life that we can use to help us develop our inner qualities. If we know what situations cause negative thoughts and feelings to arise for us we can prepare ourselves ahead of the event and then try to act or react in a positive way. If someone you know makes you feel irritated set yourself a target, try to keep your mind happy and relaxed in their presence for just one or two minutes, then if you are successful next time try for three or four minutes, eventually if you keep trying you will be able to keep away from feeling frustrated all the time. *We do not have to accept negative thoughts and emotions as inevitable, training our mind slowly but surely pulls us away from our old personality until we become someone new, someone different, someone we like to be.*

We need difficult people and challenging situations in order to train our mind. Buddhists try to view such people as being very kind as they are the rungs on our ladder to enlightenment. Buddhists believe that Buddha is constantly encouraging us to grow spiritually through bestowing blessings, which is like positive energy that helps us to change our mind and sometimes guides us into situations that we need to develop our inner qualities. Also they believe that Buddha appears in different forms, sometimes people, sometimes inanimate objects again which can help us grow. Even an illness might be a blessing in disguise if it helps us change for the better.

So a weekly list of realistic objectives is useful and as mentioned try to keep a diary of your successes, failures and conclusions and based on this develop a new set of realistic goals at the start of each week. Our success depends on being methodical and consistent in our approach so keeping good plans, strategies, goals, and records is essential. If this seems too restrictive try it both ways and see from your experience what works best for you. You will probably find that the more proactive, enthusiastic and well organized you are the better the results!

It can be very useful to develop a specific personal strategy for dealing with situations or people that cause us to develop very strong emotions like hate, rage, fear etc. If we don't plan ahead for these potential events it is easy to lose the plot and weeks of good inner work can collapse in a few minutes of intense anger or frustration. Anger is the most destructive emotion and if we are serious about training our mind we must have some strategies for overcoming it. Firstly we have to accept on a deep level that nothing positive ever comes from anger. We can still use strong words and actions in appropriate situations without feeling anger. Such strong actions do not require anger therefore anger has no useful purpose and only serves to harm us. Anger is our real enemy and when we feel it coming we have to remember this immediately in order to slow it down. Anger is such an unhappy state of mind how can it be of any benefit? What does if feel like to be angry? Anger only serves to take us away from inner peace and happiness and yet we often feel so justified when we feel it. We grasp so strongly to our own point of view and feel that the person or thing that we are angry with is inherently bad or wrong, even if it is an inanimate object like a car or computer! *It is really our own uncontrolled mind that is making us feel so discontent and unhappy.*

When we feel impatience creeping in to our mind one way to let it go is to think 'anger is my real enemy' or 'a happy mind is my best friend' or 'I accept this problem' or something similar that works for us. Gently contemplate or repeat this wise and positive thought until we feel relaxed again. This is such a wise way to manage our problems. Normally we always try to solve such problems through aggressive words or actions or by avoiding difficult people and situations but if we can train our mind like this we will just become happier and more content as we grow older. Eventually no matter what the world throws at us we will be able to deal with it positively or at least come through with less bruises.

There are many levels of anger from extreme rage to the underlying discontent that almost all humans feel throughout their lives. If we were not discontent we would not put so much energy in trying to earn more money or find better friends or partners. Discontentment is like a mild irritation or impatience in the mind that gradually destroys our inner peace. Again we can train in contentment so that we become happy with what we have.

We need to channel our discontentment in a new direction, we need to become discontent with discontent, impatient with impatience and angry with anger! Once we realize that negative thoughts and feelings are our real enemy and prevent us from experiencing happiness we can become impatient and angry with our own negative habits! Of course we have to do this with wisdom and not punish ourselves when we feel impatient with others. But this is one way of re-channeling our negative energy back on itself.

At the beginning of our training we should not expect to remain peaceful in extreme circumstances, often it is better just to walk away or avoid a situation that we know is too challenging. Or if we cannot avoid it just accept that you will feel fear or anger but know that it will not always be like this, maybe in a few months or years your mind will be stronger and you will be able to react or act in the way that you wish.

Attachment is the other side of the coin to anger. We spend all our lives trying to avoid the things we do not like and trying to obtain the things we think will bring us happiness. In this way we are constantly pulled and pushed by the minds of aversion and attachment. Attachment is more subtle than anger or aversion so it is more difficult to see why it is a problem. When we find something in this world that makes us happy our natural reaction is to become attached to it because we want that feeling of happiness to remain. Then if that something or someone is taken from us we feel anger or deep loss. The depth of our loss is at least equal to the depth of our attachment. *The more attached to something we are the greater the pain we experience when we are separated from it.* Attachment is a problem because it always gives way to pain.

Anger is an easy state of mind to recognize but attachment is not.

At the moment we may be healthy but we do not realize that we are deeply attached to our good health, if we were not we would not feel so unhappy when our body becomes ill. We take many things for granted in life and it is not until these things are taken from us that we realize how much our happiness and peace of mind depended upon them. This is why attachment is such a dangerous state of mind, it causes us to rely on things outside of our mind for our peace of mind. Imagine if someone close to you died or you lost your job or you discovered you had cancer, how would you feel? Of course you would feel lots of unpleasant emotions but all this comes from attachment.

It takes a long time to let go of attachment, we have to accept this and work at it gradually by constantly reminding ourselves that the things we are attached to are transitory and it is inevitable that we will be separated from them one day, nothing lasts in this world. If we think like this slowly over months and years we will let go in our mind. Letting go of attachment doesn't mean abandoning our friends or family or wealth but simply changing our outlook. If we let go in our mind now when we are inevitably parted from the people and things we like it will be much easier for us. Less attachment means less pain and far more genuine happiness.

The other wonderful thing about nonattachment is the sense of freedom we feel. The less we need other people and things the freer and lighter and more flexible we feel. Natural happiness from within is much purer and reliable than artificial happiness that comes from attachment. Also our love for others becomes stronger and purer as we become less dependent and conditional in our relationships, so in this sense nonattachment actually causes us to draw closer to others and become a better friend, partner, parent, child etc.

Again we can use simple affirmations and meditations to

help us overcome attachment. Success comes from regularity of contemplation and meditation, if we don't find time for this in our daily routine nothing will change. Think in term of months and years, plan ahead, think 'What do I want the rest of my life to be like? Is there some value in these ideas? Do I want my mind to get weaker and more attached to this world as I grow older? What kind of person do I want to be in ten years time?' *We need to ask ourselves honest, powerful and searching questions in order to stimulate our inner growth.*

Working on our attachment also helps us to overcome our anger, as we only get angry if we are attached to something. We get angry in queues because we want to be first and we feel that our time is more important than others'. We get angry in all kinds of situations because we are attached to our own happiness, but eventually through training our mind we can become attached to the happiness of others through developing the special mind of love or compassion and then we will be naturally happy all the time. Being attached to the happiness of others through compassion means that we use our wisdom and help them in the best way possible at any particular time and that might not always mean being 'nice' but always means being kind.

Finally a few reminders! One of the best ways of developing a realistic plan is to keep a diary for a year. Buy a blank diary and keep a record of your ups and downs on the spiritual path and this will help you to keep going long term. The other benefit of this is that you can see yourself changing by looking back a few months and remembering how you were when you first started. Split your day up mentally, if things go wrong you can take a break then start afresh at the next section of the day, i.e. morning, afternoon, evening. Keep things simple, if you don't have time to meditate just make a positive intention at the start of each day, and eventually even at the start of each 'section' of the day.

There are two more simple things we can do to make our training more powerful and protect it from degenerating. The first is to have a good reason or motivation for what we are doing and to remember it as often as possible. If we sincerely think and feel 'may all living beings benefit from this inner training' or 'may this inner training be a cause of lasting happiness for all living beings' this kind of intention changes everything. We cannot begin to imagine what good karma we create by consistently keeping such an altruistic motivation, and if this is our sincere wish it will become a reality, our practice of becoming a better person will become a powerful cause of happiness for others.

Buddhists in the Mahayana tradition try to keep a special motivation of Bodhichitta when training the mind; this is a wish to attain enlightenment knowing that it is the best way to help others. *If we become enlightened we can help others in many ways that currently we cannot comprehend.* So whenever they engage in mind training or any positive thought or action they do so with the intention 'may I become a Buddha for the benefit of all'. Having a positive intention like this directs our good energy or karma toward the end result that we want to achieve.

The second helpful addition to our daily practice is the mental action of dedicating the positive energy or good karma of positive mental or physical actions. Dedication is similar to intention but it comes after the action. We can dedicate or direct our good karma at the end of the day or several times a day or as often as we like. Just take some time to remember why you are training your mind and generate a positive thought like 'I dedicate all my positive actions to world peace' or ' I dedicate all my positive actions to the lasting happiness of all living beings' or whatever you feel is a good goal. The more altruistic we make our motivation and dedication the more powerful our good karma becomes and this naturally gives us more energy to advance along our path of personal and spiritual growth.

Avoid anything that takes you away from your inner training unless you are ready to transform it into the path. We do need challenges so don't walk away just because you cannot be bothered or one day you will regret not using your time to develop your mind. *Remember you do not have to go anywhere, or do anything, or be with anyone to be happy, you can just be happy.* Generally we look for happiness in the wrong place and eventually through training your mind you will find it quite easily from within.

Be honest with your progress or lack of it, be realistic and keep a sense of humor. Develop a support network of like-minded people, find a meditation class (appendix 1). Don't get wrapped up in yourself, there are countless people struggling to survive and find a little happiness. Think of them and grasp this opportunity to make a difference to the world. Don't try to convert others but inspire them through your own example of what a human being can become.

The essential points from this chapter are:

You can change, all you need is a realistic plan and a consistent wish. Acceptance is the first step towards inner change. If we cannot change something that is making us unhappy we have to accept things as they are, then in time we can train our mind and learn to be happy whatever our external problems.

A positive thought or some meditation at the start of every day can make a big difference to our quality of life. Try to be aware of the quality of your thoughts and emotions throughout the rest of the day and from time to time try to reaffirm the positive start you made.

Don't give up, training your mind is like being a good parent, some days be firm with yourself and some days gentle encouragement is best. Don't be afraid to make mistakes and don't be hard on yourself when you do. Keep trying and you will be successful, give up and nothing will change.

Exercise:

Make a list of all the things that make you feel angry, frustrated or impatient, even the little things. Make a realistic plan for using these opportunities to train your mind. Start with the small stuff, set yourself some challenges for the next seven days. For example when you are in a traffic queue decide to stay relaxed and calm for the first ten minutes or whatever pushes your mind a little beyond its usual limits! In this way you are training the mental muscle of patience.

Now try a meditation:

When your mind has settled down develop a good intention like 'may every living being benefit from this meditation'. Spend a few minutes doing the gentle breathing meditation explained in chapter 4. Then meditate using the following contemplation:

Try to bring to mind all the opportunities in your life for training your mind. Think about all the situations and people that you have to deal with on a daily basis that bring out the worst in you! Understanding what you have already learnt from this book, try to come to the conclusion that these people and situations are exactly what you need to grow, they are like a mirror showing what parts of your mind you need to work on and they are like a the mountain for the mountaineer. Without learning to use these challenging situations we will never become a better person. Meditate on this conclusion, focus on the wish to use challenging situations to become a better person.

When you have finished, make a short dedication like 'through the power of these positives thoughts may all living beings find lasting happiness' and try to carry your positive thoughts into the rest of the day.

Use this page to make some notes on what you found thought-provoking or useful in this chapter:

6

OVERCOMING STRESS

After reading this chapter you should be able to:

Understand the causes of stress

Begin the process of reducing stress

Have some practical solutions to everyday problems

Stress is one of the major problems of the modern world, particularly in the west. We have all suffered from it at one time or another, sometimes it is caused by relationship problems or money, sometimes by the pace of life that we lead. Many people have demanding careers and feel that they cannot afford to relax or someone else will get the promotion. Sometimes we are driven to work long hours to pay for the mortgage or school fees or the new car. Of course we all want a good standard of living and there is nothing wrong in striving to achieve our ambitions but we have to be careful and check that what we are doing will bring us what we want in our hearts.

Of course wherever we find ourselves in life we can transform our situation by changing our outlook but sometimes there is no point in remaining in a dull job when you could find greater freedom and satisfaction leading a different way of life. Many people find themselves in jobs or careers that they cannot leave because there is no practical alternative and in those situations we need to apply our understanding of mind training to use the situation to help us change for the better. But if we have the opportunity to change and we do not take it, why? If you commute to work every day look at the people around you, many people look stressed, depressed or just lost, it looks like these people are dying a little everyday. What more evidence do we need? We have to train our mind or make an external change that will help us to grow as a human being. If that means living a better quality of life with less money then so be it, if it means moving to a smaller house, buying a second hand car instead of a new one then so be it. *We have to choose a way of life that makes us feel alive, that makes us want to live.* Sometimes too much external comfort encourages us to be dull, we lose our edge, we lose our vitality and we stop growing. Although this is not a rule because we can be poor and lack any wish to grow or we can be rich and lead a very full and meaningful life. Mainly we have to be clear that our external environment and the way we are living is not holding us back from leading a more meaningful life. Sometimes it can be helpful to change our external environment and circle of friends in order to help support our inner growth. We have to use our own wisdom and judgment and don't try to transform what is beyond our capacity and be courageous enough to make the changes needed to help us develop our new life.

So if we want to overcome stress we can make some external changes. But mainly stress is an inner problem, it comes from within us and that is where we will also find the cure. If the main cause of stress was external factors then everyone who had the same level of difficult external circumstances would have the same level of stress. Because this is not true it indicates that external factors contribute to stress but are not the main cause. We probably know from our own experience that sometimes we have dealt with potentially stressful situations in a strong and confident way and felt no lasting mental discomfort and probably at other times in our life we have been overwhelmed by apparently insignificant external problems. So again we can tell from this that our level of stress is directly related to our state of mind, if we are generally a strong and confident person we do not experience much stress. A useful place to start is to acknowledge that we can change, we do not have to accept that we will always be susceptible to stress. *Just knowing that we can change can make us feel stronger.*

I remember being at school and witnessing a gang of boys tormenting another boy in a cloakroom. This happened almost every day to the same boy, mainly because he was nervous and weak minded and other boys knew he would never retaliate. This particular day a teacher came in and cleared everyone out of the cloakroom apart from the victim, for some reason I and another friend hid behind a   pile of coats! We heard the teacher asking the boy about what had happened, he just broke down in tears. The teacher stayed with him until he had let go of all his emotion and then said to him, 'this will carry on for the rest of your life unless you change now'. The teacher and the boy left and my friend and I breathed a sigh of relief that we had not been found. This incident stays in my mind because from that day onward the boy changed completely, he became the most confident, outgoing, strong, and vital person in our class. The last time I met him we were both about twenty eight years old and he was still the same, full of confidence and genuinely full of life.

This was an unusual event, I think there was only one other time when I saw it happen to someone else, but it proves that deep inner change is possible if we are ready to completely let go of who we are and become someone new. Generally we change gradually and this is as it should be because it generally leads to lasting change. Dealing with stress is just the same, if we expect to become a continually happy, confident and relaxed individual overnight we are being unrealistic, but if we plan our ascent on 'Mount Stress' and we prepare well and take things step by step we are guaranteed to succeed. I think we can safely use the word 'guaranteed' because as mentioned, training our mind or improving our personality is just like training or improving our body; if we go to the gym every week we are guaranteed to become stronger and fitter. Of course our body becomes fitter if we exercise, it is just a simple matter of cause and effect. Scientific studies have shown that our intellectual mind improves the more we use it, but this is also the case with our feelings and emotions as they are just another aspect of our mind. We can improve our memory by using it, we can improve our ability to solve problems by problem-solving, we can improve our concentration by concentrating more and so on. Once we accept this it is easy to see that if we want to be happy, relaxed and confident it can be done, we just have to exercise those parts of our mind on a regular basis. *Just by developing familiarity with inner peace, confidence and compassion these states of mind will become easier and easier to develop.* But if we do not put the time and effort in, especially in the first few weeks and months, there will be no long-term change.

Understanding this can give us real enthusiasm because we know through the power of our own mind we can overcome stress and anxiety, we just have to accept where we are at the moment, plan ahead and take things step by step at our own pace. It is great to know that we do not have to accept a future of stress and anxiety; we can be free of these barriers to happiness in our mind. It can be useful to think of negative states of mind as 'barriers' to happiness because this helps you to separate the negative mind from you as a person. Often we feel that we are naturally a stressful or anxious or angry person rather than thinking 'stress is a barrier to happiness in my mind' or 'anger is a barrier to happiness in my mind'. It is very difficult to let go of these states of mind when we feel that we 'are' them or that they 'are' us.

Obviously we are not anger or stress, these experiences in our mind are just like passing clouds in the sky, clouds are not the sky. If we were stress we would always be stressful but this is not so, we all experience moments of peace, or less stress than normal! This tells us that stress is not permanent, it can change, it can sometimes disappear altogether. This will be our experience if we train our mind to let go of stress and become familiar with the 'clear blue sky' of inner peace. Even if it takes a long time it is still worth beginning this journey now because if we do not do anything things will just get worse. In some ways we have no choice, sooner or later we all have to begin this journey.

Think about how much stress you have already experienced in this life, not to mention previous lives! If we could add it all up it would be a mountain of negativity. How has this production of negativity helped us or helped the world? Stress is completely useless, it harms us and it is just more negative energy in a world that is crying out for peaceful people. *If we don't make an effort to change our world will not change, we are adding to the problems of our world.* All the stress we have produced and experienced in the past has just been wasted time in our life, there was no need for it, it didn't help us in anyway but only made us miserable. If we think like this we will come to view stress as our enemy and every time it begins to appear in our mind we will see it for what it is and want to destroy it. This is the kind of attitude we need to successfully overcome stress, we need to be very clear in our mind that feelings of stress are our enemy and a barrier to happiness.

Once we have identified the enemy clearly we will spot it as soon as it starts to attack us and we can immediately retaliate. However at the moment we are probably doing just the opposite, we are probably inviting the enemy in to our mind and asking him to make himself at home! Then we give him a hearty meal by allowing our mind to dwell on the difficult problems we are having. Of course if we do this our enemy becomes stronger and stronger and never leaves our mind. At the moment we are probably not even asking him politely to leave because we do not think he is the problem. *We think the problem is outside our mind -our job, our marriage, our neighbor, our health - but the problem is inside our mind, the problem is always our state of mind.*

So the first practical step in overcoming stress is to practice watching our mind and identifying at the earliest possible moment the beginnings of stressful feelings or thoughts. It doesn't matter if we cannot stop them, we have taken the first steps forward, we have fired a warning shot at stress. We could do this even for a few weeks before we take the next step. One of the things we need to do is be very practical and work within our own capability. We have to accept it will take time to change and if we settle in to this idea and take the pressure off ourselves to overcome stress this is another victory, we have fired another warning shot at stress, now he is getting worried! To help you be persistent in your mind training you may find it helpful to write this down and put it somewhere you will see it every day:

IF I APPLY EFFORT AND ENTHUSIAM, WITHOUT EXPECTATION, FOR AS LONG AS IT TAKES, I AM GUARANTEED SUCCESS.

The next thing we need to do is to build into our personal plan strategies for dealing with failure! Of course we are going to make mistakes and have days when we feel our old self is as strong as ever but if we are prepared these will not be such great obstacles for us. As mentioned we will probably have lots of energy and enthusiasm for inner change to begin with but we have to prepare for when this runs out. It might be after a few days, weeks, or months. We might be able to guess from experience what our threshold is for enthusiasm. We have probably made New Year resolutions, how long have we kept them? Usually enthusiasm starts to ebb away slowly, almost imperceptibly at first, until one day we realize we have completely forgotten our good intentions and we have to start all over again. This is why planning, routine and consistency are the keys to success in transforming our mind.

Again if we write everything down, make realistic and inspiring plans, formulate a steady, practical routine for inner transformation that we can stick to and keep a diary of our success and 'failure' and use this to create a new plan every week we are really putting our self in control. Starting small and building slowly is a very wise way to begin and taking breaks, especially in the first few months, is very helpful. If we feel it is too daunting we do not have to develop a plan that means trying to be positive every day! Try every other day to begin with or take one or two days off from 'the plan' every week and just let your mind relax. Your mind is much more likely to follow you if you are well balanced in your approach, which just means working within your capacity, not being too lazy or too hard on yourself.

When we feel our enthusiasm start to ebb we need to regenerate it, enthusiasm is just a state of mind, like sadness or stress or kindness. What made us enthusiastic in the first place? If you are feeling enthusiastic now, why? Is it the prospect of a new start, a new life or the feeling that you have the power to transform your life? Whatever the reasons write them down. Then as soon as you feel yourself slipping away from enthusiasm use your notes and memory to bring you back. Sometimes we might need to do this regularly for a few days before we regain our energy to continue, which is fine, just try to feel that this is not a set back but just part of your path. Then the next time it happens you will know what to do and it will probably pass a little quicker. In this way we build our enthusiasm or mental energy for inner transformation over time, it is an aspect of our personality that we need to build just like an athlete has to build up certain muscles for their particular sport. *We won't succeed without enthusiasm so we have to build it steadily, like an emotional muscle, so it becomes strong and consistent.*

Again this is not something we can do overnight so we have to expect periods where we lack enthusiasm. Probably over time we will come to gradually realize that if we want freedom from stress or we want to find lasting happiness we have to accept that the path of inner growth or transformation is one of the most important things in our life because it colors every other aspect of our life. If we feel well inside, if we feel at peace with our past, content in the present and confident in our future this state of mind makes every aspect of our life good. Over time we will feel that this is where we want to go then our enthusiasm will become deep and stable and bring great results.

So don't expect to change on a deep level quickly, if you have been prone to stress for years expecting this to change overnight is unrealistic. It is easier for some people to change than others so we have to build into our plan an expectation of failure according to the kind of person we are and what we think we can realistically achieve. By doing this we will combat frustration when we find ourselves acting out old habits and ensure longevity in training our mind.

As mentioned earlier it can be helpful to write down a detailed list of the things that make you feel stressed, the things, situations and people. When we see it in black and white and make a specific plan of action to deal with these things again this can make us feel empowered, encouraged and in control. Again it doesn't matter if we fail, we are trying and that in itself is a little victory, in time we will fail less and less and eventually conquer stress. There is no rush or race, this is an important thing to take seriously and do well just like any other important project in life.

Write the list in order of severity with the most severe at the top. Now we need to train from the bottom up. Start with the least severe situation that causes the lowest level of stress. On a clean sheet of paper write down clearly how you feel approaching, during and after this experience of stress. How long do the feelings of stress last, how do you feel mentally, emotionally and physically?

Then write down on the same sheet under a different heading how you would like to react in an ideal world, if you could change completely overnight what kind of person you would like to be and how you would feel and react differently. Just let your imagination take you to a different place and enjoy being that person for a few minutes, this is almost like drawing a blueprint of the person you would like to be. Then again under a new heading write down a realistic goal that will take you one step away from your old self and one step toward your imagined self. If might be something like, 'the next time I have to give a speech I will stay relaxed and calm up to 24 hours before the event' or 'the next time I have a meeting with this person I will remain calm for the first five minutes' or 'the next time I am in a traffic jamb I will be relaxed for the first five minutes' or 'the next time I am short of money I will happily accept this for one day'.

To begin with choose a few things from the bottom of the list and make a corresponding list of realistic goals. If you feel able you can do this for the whole list so that you are attacking stress from every possible angle in your life, but again don't take on too much, it is better to start slowly and steadily. When you have a list of realistic goals you need to look at each one carefully and think, 'what can I do to put myself in the best possible position to achieve this goal?' Again we need to be like an athlete or business executive and be completely ruthless with stress. Just like an army commander never underestimates his enemy but plans for any eventuality we need to be methodical, farsighted and focused. By having this attitude we are really taking the power away from stress because we have a strong intention to control the situation. The stronger that intention the less energy there is for stress to survive. *Stress needs our mental energy or attention to survive, by focusing our mind on overcoming stress we are cutting off its air supply.*

If our mind is 100% focused on a deep feeling of inner peace it is impossible for stress to live in our mind it goes completely. Obviously it takes considerable time and effort to achieve this but if we keep our final goal in mind from time to time it can help to remind us that stress only exists because we create it. It is like rubbish in the mind, you would not allow someone to empty a bag of rubbish in your house and yet we do this everyday in our mind!

Again it can be helpful to start every week with a plan, you can put your goals in your diary or keep a separate diary just for this purpose. At the end of each day just spend a few minutes recording how you reacted in different situations, did you achieve your aims? To what extent, 50%, 75%? Then briefly plan ahead for the next day. At the end of the week take a little time to see what you have achieved and plan ahead for the next week.

How can we transform a specific stressful situation in to a cause of inner peace or freedom from stress? To begin we just need to develop a strong intention to do this, then we need to plan ahead so that when the situation arises we are prepared as much as possible. We also need some experience of watching our mind so that we can act as soon as we feel the first signs of stress. Then as mentioned earlier we need to let go of those initial feelings of anxiety or nervousness and allow our mind to relax and try to 'hold' or stay with that relaxed feeling throughout the difficult situation. Initially we may not be able to do this at all, we may only be able to spot the first feelings of stress but not stop them growing in to a fully stressful experience. This can be demoralizing if we are not prepared for it. But just recognizing the first signs of stress is a big step forward. It doesn't matter if we cannot go further than this for weeks or even months, we have made a significant start and should be pleased with this. Our next significant goal might be to stay relaxed for a little longer or to not allow the initial feelings of stress to grow for just a few minutes. *Each time we take a small manageable step we are attacking stress, if continued over time the enemy will be defeated, no doubt.* To begin with we will take small steps and it won't feel like we are making significant progress, but we are because those initial small steps are the foundations of the larger steps to come. With small victories our confidence, strength and skill will increase and in time we will be able to make greater progress. We will become a wise inner warrior.

Sometimes stress arises in our mind because of aimless worry and not because of a specific stressful situation and again we need to apply the same technique. As soon as we recognize that our mind is beginning to dwell on negative thoughts and emotions we need to remind our self that it is that mental action of dwelling on problems that is making us unhappy. Again try to drop those thoughts and feelings and replace them with positive ones. We can do this through the power of affirmations or by doing a little breathing meditation or sometimes just through the power of logical reasoning. We can think 'by allowing my mind to dwell on this problem I am making myself unhappy'. There are many ways we can pull ourselves away from negative thoughts and emotions so we need to be creative and try to find the techniques that work for us. Sometimes just going for a walk can help or calling a friend and talking about your problems for a short time to get things off your chest, but make sure you are not using this as an excuse to focus on your problems. Even better focus your mind on helping someone else, this can really help us to stop feeling 'my problems are the only problems in the world'.

Learning to consciously relax is a skill that we all need and it is the key to overcoming stress. If we learn the simple meditation technique in chapter 4 this will give us a great head start. Again we need to take our time and don't expect too much too soon, but often you will feel a big difference in your quality of life within a few weeks if you practice a little meditation every day. When we practice this meditation on a regular basis we will come to know through our own experience how to relax and then we can apply this experience to any situation in life. It is much easier to be happy when we are able to mentally and physically relax. In time we can maintain this sense of inner peace even when we are physically or mentally busy. Stress is not useful in any way, in fact just the opposite, when we are stressed we cannot think clearly or creatively and even our physical actions become clumsy and erratic. *A clear, calm and peaceful mind makes all our inner and outer activities more enjoyable and effective.*

Avoiding stressful situations is fine if we are not ready to cope with them but it is not a long-term answer, at some point we have to admit that a certain amount of courage is needed if we are to progress. We also need to expect some discomfort in the form of fear or anxiety when we face up to stressful situations for the first time and recognize that these feelings are not failure. Failure means not trying at all.

We might need a 'feel the fear and do it anyway' kind of attitude to start with. If we can think that stressful situations are opportunities to grow rather than things to avoid we will be more able to accept a little discomfort, just like a mountaineer accepts discomfort as part of her challenge to conquer the mountain. Again there is no good reason to take on too much too soon as this will just hamper our progress, we need to learn our limitations and work within them until we are ready to push beyond them.

Finally it can be very helpful to remember that we are not here forever! A human life is really quite brief in the great scheme of things, even if we live to a ripe old age our time on earth goes quickly. It is important to be happy while we are here and to do something with our life that we feel has some meaning. It is much easier to die with a happy mind when we feel that we have lived well and it is very sad when people die with a mind of confusion or regret. Remembering our own mortality helps us to let go of stress because we realize it is just wasted time and it helps us to focus our mind on what we feel has some meaning or purpose.

The essential points from this chapter are:

Stress serves no useful purpose; it just makes a difficult situation worse. It is possible to live a life without stress just by learning to train our mind to be relaxed and happy. Of course this takes time but if we take this task seriously we are guaranteed success. Learn to watch your mind and spot stress at the earliest stages before it becomes too large to control. Talk to yourself: 'If I allow these feelings of stress to grow I will feel very unhappy', try to relax and let go of the tension or worry, try a little meditation. If you cannot do this try to distract your mind with something positive, phone a friend and take an interest in their problems, do a helpful job for a neighbor, anything that takes your attention away from your own problems and makes you feel good about yourself.

Exercise:

Think of the things that normally make you feel stressed, choose one and then deliberately put yourself in that stressful situation. Use this as an opportunity to watch your mind, make a note of how you feel leading up to, during and after the event. Then do the same thing again but this time plan ahead and use all your skill to overcome the stress. Again make a note of your feelings and you will find that even though you have not trained your mind for a long time just through the power of your will you can reduce the impact of stress in your life.

Meditation:

When your mind has settled down develop a good intention like 'may every living being benefit from this meditation'. Spend a few minutes doing the gentle breathing meditation explained in chapter 4. Then meditate using the following contemplation:

Think about all the times in your life when you have felt under severe stress. Take some time to vividly remember the situations and the worry, fear or depression that you felt. Then ask yourself if those negative feelings served any useful purpose. Try to come to a powerful conclusion that life is precious and such feelings are just wasted time, then concentrate on the wish to be free from stress in the future.

When you have finished make a short dedication like 'through the power of these positive thoughts may all living beings find lasting happiness' and try to carry your positive thoughts into the rest of the day.

Use this page to make some notes on what you found thought-provoking or useful in this chapter:

7

BETTER RELATIONSHIPS

After reading this chapter you should be able to:

Understand the main causes of relationship problems

Look at relationships from a new perspective

Apply some practical ideas and solutions

Relationships are one of the main sources of happiness for human beings; good relationships are vital if we want to be happy. This is obviously true because we know that so much stress and unhappiness comes from relationship problems and breakdowns. We all have many different types of relationships, most of us are part of a family so we have a certain number of close relationships in that environment, we might have a partner or children, brothers, sisters, parents, aunts and uncles. At work we probably have a whole new set of relationships and then there are friends and neighbors and the list goes on. So in our life we probably have maybe 50 to 200 people who we relate to on a regular basis on different levels. Each one of these people are in a similar network of relationships. If we have a good relationship with someone we have the opportunity to touch the lives of all the people they have a close relationship with. ***If we are a good partner, friend, work colleague and family member our life can be a real force for good in the world.***

We are not islands; our destiny is caught up with the destiny of all living beings, not just the ones in this small world! Whatever we do, even the quality of our thoughts and feelings, affects the whole of this vast web of existence. If we feel that we are part of something much larger than our self this can be very mind expanding it can help to broaden our field of concern to include all living beings not just those that we currently regard as special to us. This attitude of wisdom enriches all our relationships because we start to feel that the happiness of all living beings is important, not just our own. This sense of care or responsibility is the key to better relationships. The main cause of problems in relationships is self-concern, we have expectations and when they are not met we become unhappy and sometimes angry and even violent.

Somehow we need to take a leap in consciousness and begin to love others without expectation. A good example of this is the love that a parent has for their children, sometimes children are naughty but the parent always has a mind of love. A good parent always wants what is best for the child and if that means making sacrifices they are often happy to do this and when the child has grown up and is ready to leave home the parent lets go and is happy because their children are happy. It is possible to cultivate this kind of love toward everyone so that we are no longer a slave to our own wishes. It is when our own wishes are not fulfilled by others that we become unhappy and angry. *We are so attached to our own happiness that our mind is easily disturbed when others do not do what we want.*

As mentioned earlier, at the moment our quality of life depends very much on having a comfortable external environment. To maintain a sense of contentment we need a good job, a good partner, a good income, clothes, car, house etc. If we suddenly lost some of these our mental and emotional world would collapse. Because we have spent all our time cultivating a comfortable external world our internal world is very weak and susceptible to the ups and downs of life. Our dependence on others forms a big part of this fragility and potential for suffering. Since it is inevitable that sooner or later we will be parted from the people and things that make us happy it makes sense to get ready. Just in the same way that we prepare for old age by having a pension and health insurance we can prepare for the inevitable challenges ahead by letting go of our attachment to people, places and possessions.

Letting go is a state of mind. We do not have to change anything on a physical level. When we let go on a deep level we experience a sense of freedom, inner peace and contentment. This inner freedom allows us to enjoy life even more. Far from being depressed because we know we will have to let go of these things we are happy because we know these things are in the nature of change. Being in touch and feeling the changing nature of all things gives us freedom and peace of mind.

Take some time out to think about this, is it true, is everything in the nature of change? Does anything remain the same for more than a moment? Even solid objects like cars and houses and mountains are changing moment by moment. Obviously these things change more slowly than things like the weather but still they are part of the great ocean of impermanence. We may accept this on an intellectual level but it is not until we actually start to feel it that this wisdom can have a profound effect on our quality of life. When we start to feel that everything is impermanent then we start to let go. We develop less dependence on people and places and things, and this brings a sense of peace and space within our mind. *Feeling the impermanence of life gives us a sense of freedom, we are free from grasping at things as permanent.*

It is this mind of grasping at permanence that causes most of our problems in life. We get so caught up in the world and take things so seriously that when things go wrong we get really hurt or disappointed. We get so caught up and captivated by the external world because we have forgotten its changing nature, we feel and act as if people, places and possessions are permanent. Because of this belief we put all our time and energy into creating a comfortable environment, finding good relationships, making money and before we know it our life is drawing to a close and all that we have worked for is falling through our fingers.

As mentioned before many eastern cultures believe that the meaning of a human life is to become a better human being, to develop spiritually, to become wiser, kinder, more content and compassionate, to develop a deeper understanding of life and to try to help others in any way we can. But by forgetting that we and others and our world are impermanent we do just the opposite. We know that human beings are capable of leading very inspiring and rewarding lives, we are all capable of great acts of kindness and yet so many people just choose a material approach to life never even glimpsing the possibility of becoming a better person or making some lasting contribution to the welfare of others.

If we were rich and we knew that the person next door was starving to death we would definitely be moved to help them. *In this global village everyone is our neighbor, their happiness is our responsibility.* It is easy to make donations to charities that we know are directly helping others in danger of starvation and yet we choose to buy another new car! In this sense our relationship with others is very childish because we think much more about ourselves than we do about others who really need our help. How can we say that we are part of an advanced society or a Christian country when we turn our back on others? When 20% of the world's population own 80% of the wealth and this state of affairs does not change over time we are not accepting our responsibility. In this sense there is nothing heroic or superior about our society, again just the opposite, we are psychologically and spiritually still children.

Developing a feeling of impermanence is a way to help us get our lives back on track and improve our relationships. If our doctor told us that we only had a few months to live how would that change our relationships? We would probably let go of all the minor arguments and annoyances we had with others and every day would become a special event because we were aware that soon we would be permanently parted from others. Yet we cannot be sure that we will be alive next week, often young people die before their parents, even as you read this book your body may be developing a serious illness that you do not yet know about. Even if we live to be eighty our life will pass quickly, ask any old person and they will often say, 'I don't know where the time has gone'.

So feeling impermanence teaches us that we do not have time to waste on petty squabbles, it makes us feel that time and life are precious. Feeling impermanence changes our personality for the better, it helps us mature, it helps us to relax and let go of striving for happiness in the external world and focus on things that have some meaning. Feeling impermanence helps us to value relationships without becoming attached to them. Understanding impermanence allows us to enjoy deep and fulfilling relationships but also allows us the freedom to let people go when the relationship comes to a natural end. Since we will be parted from everyone we know and everything we own it does not make sense to cling on to others. It is this emotional need or attachment that causes us the pain when we are parted from others, it is like a mental glue which attaches us to the other person because we feel we need this person in our life to maintain our happiness. When looked at like this we can see that attachment is completely selfish and just the opposite of love. ***Attachment is motivated by the need to fulfill only our own happiness whereas love is only concerned with the happiness of others.***

Most of the time our relationships are a mixture of love and attachment but over time we can learn how to reduce our attachment and increase our mind of pure love. A mind of pure love is a very mature mind, very light, flexible, relaxed and happy and people who possess this mind are delighted to help others, in fact their main source of happiness comes from their love for others. Having a mind of love toward others does not mean that we have to go around hugging everyone, love is just a state of mind. We can express this love in our words and actions but it is better just to be normal in our behavior and not too over the top, unless that is our natural personality!

Our own desires and wishes are endless, if we try to find lasting happiness by fulfilling them we will never succeed. There will always be something more that we feel we need. At some point in our life we have to grow up and accept this on a deep level. We know happiness and contentment are just a state of mind, just an inner experience. To try to generate this inner experience by collecting all the external things that we feel we must have to be happy is a very complicated and precarious route to take. We have to accept that this path is doomed to failure because it depends upon so many fluctuating factors. Good relationships are just one of the many things that most humans need to feel happy, supported and secure. But we know that this one thing is so unpredictable and often just plain hard work. Our moods change quickly, the moods of our friends and family change quickly, we often get bored or irritated with others and visa versa. Finding stable and lasting happiness in the external world is an impossible game to win.

Love is a much simpler and guaranteed path to inner peace, deep happiness and successful relationships. How can we start to walk this new inner path to happiness? To begin with we need to realize where we are at present and start our journey step by step from that point.

At present we all have a very strong sense of 'I' or 'me', most of our thoughts and emotions are focused on ourselves. We think about our own happiness almost all the time but we rarely think about the welfare of others. We might feel that we love our friends and family but even this love is mixed with strong attachment. This strong attachment is based on a strong sense of 'I'. If we did not have a strong sense of self-importance we would not have such strong attachment and our relationships would be much smoother and simpler.

This strong sense of 'I' makes us feel that our happiness is the most important, it makes us feel that we are the centre of the universe and everything revolves around us. When our sense of 'I' is very strong we feel that our point of view is correct and we are completely closed to the thoughts and feelings of others. Our sense of 'I' or self-grasping can be quite a difficult thing to see in our own mind. It is much easier to see or feel when we are experiencing an extreme state of mind like anger, fear, embarrassment, jealousy, depression, loneliness, etc. When we have these states of mind all our attention is focused on our self, on our own problems and difficult situation. At that time we are not thinking about others, all our mental energy is pointing inwards and actually making our problems much bigger.

Behind all extreme negative states of mind there is a strong sense of 'I'. If we can learn to reduce and finally let go of this sense of self-importance we will be completely free from all kinds of problems and unhappiness forever. This is a big job but it is not as frightening as it sounds, in fact when we let go of our 'I' we experience a wonderful sense of freedom and natural happiness that our 'I' has been preventing us from enjoying.

Before we can completely let go of our 'I' we need to put much time and effort in to reducing it. The more we can reduce it the happier we become so this is a really worthwhile venture. The way to gradually reduce our deeply rooted sense of self-importance is to use situations that naturally cause us to develop a strong sense of 'I' and steadily work towards reducing our sense of 'I' in these situations. If we avoid these situations we are not actually solving the underlying problem, the spiritual path is a middle way between not avoiding challenging situations and not allowing our self to be overwhelmed or carried away by them. By following this path we learn how to control our mind, which brings great inner peace and confidence.

Relationships are a good place to begin because they often cause us to develop a strong sense of 'I' very easily. This is fantastic because now our relationship problems can become the cause of developing good relationships! As mentioned before we need challenging people and situations to help us grow, to help us become better people. Like the mountaineer we need a mountain. Relationships cause us to feel negative minds like irritation, anger, jealousy, attachment, desire, loneliness, low self esteem and low confidence; now looking at this from a fresh perspective we are being given the opportunity to develop the opposite positive states of mind like patience, kindness, contentment, love, confidence, happiness and inner peace.

Basically our relationship problems are just our own negative states of mind! Of course there are many ways relationships can improve through better communication and empathy from both sides. But our basic problem is our own mind. In the long run we cannot rely on others to change in order that we can remain happy and content. In order to find lasting happiness we need to go straight to the source of the problem, our own mind, and begin our journey from there. There needs to be a fundamental change in our attitude towards relationships, we need to view relationships as opportunities to grow, learn and give. Generally we feel just the opposite, often it seems that relationships are there just to take away our loneliness or to give us some excitement or comfort.

Whenever we encounter a relationship problem, either with a close member of our family, someone at work, or just the people we meet on a daily basis, we need to get in to the habit of seeing these problems as opportunities. For a mountaineer the mountain is more an opportunity than a problem and because of this attitude her will to succeed is very strong. In the same way if we change our attitude our will to succeed will become strong and that is half the battle.

When we encounter problems in our relationships we need to take some time out and reflect on the real causes and practical solutions. Decide not to follow your usual pattern of thinking, feeling and acting. Just say to the other person involved 'I need some time to think about this'. This time is very helpful because it gives us the mental space to look at the possibilities of a new way of reacting internally and externally. Often we get into patterns of behavior in all aspects of life and especially in relationships, so to take a new direction after years of habitual behavior takes planning and effort but can be very rewarding.

When we have found a little space and time to examine our

relationship problem we first need to be honest with our self and look at our own mind. Ask yourself a question 'how do I normally react to this kind of problem'? This in itself may induce a wish to act differently and we should try to hold this wish in our mind and allow it grow, meditate on it, encourage it, try to vividly imagine how your life would be better if you reacted to relationship problems in a much more open and positive way. If we do this on a regular basis it won't be too long before we create enough mental and emotional momentum for real inner change.

At the moment we mainly view relationships as one of the many things we need to keep happy. We mainly seek relationships for our own selfish needs, consequently we try to spend as much time as possible with people we like, people who make us feel good, and as little time as possible with people we do not like. In this way our relationships are based on a very introverted and selfish foundation, we are mainly taking from others rather than giving. Generally we get into relationships because we think we can get something out of them, we rarely enter any kind of relationship because we feel we have something to enrich the life of another human being. *All our relationship problems arise because we are so wrapped up in our own search for happiness, there is really very little space in our mind for others.* Just understanding and accepting this is a big step forward. At present our happiness depends so much on the way other people behave that we constantly live on a knife-edge. Yet all we have to do is to let go of expectation, change inside, accept others as they are and our mind will relax and we will find some inner peace.

Again we will never find the lasting happiness we wish for by relying on the changing fortunes of life. People come and go, relationships come and go, this is the nature of our world, everything around us is constantly changing, even our own life will come to an end one day. If we can start to accept this our life will be much more enjoyable. If we can combine this acceptance with a sincere wish for others to be happy, a mind of love, then all our relationship problems will disappear. *The more we love others the less self concern we have and the happier we become, lose yourself in love and you will be completely happy.*

It is because we do not love that we are unhappy and our relationships are turbulent. The world we live in does not encourage or value love, on the contrary we are brought up to believe that we need to look after number one. This is ironic because this attitude often comes from our parents, because they love us they want us to be happy and not to suffer so they encourage us to look after our self, to put our self first, to do well in our education and career, to find the right job and good relationships. Consequently we grow up feeling that our happiness is the most important in the world, but this attitude actually stops us from experiencing real inner peace and lasting happiness! We are so focused on our own happiness that we find it very difficult to even empathize with others let alone develop the wish to give practical help. Because many individuals are like this, whole countries are like this, as a country we become very defensive and suspicious, we are reluctant to give aid unless there is something in it for us, we are reluctant to take action on ecological issues unless others do it first, we are even prepared to solve our problems by going to war and destroying others. So the world we live in has many problems which all come down to the mind of self-concern and sense of 'I'.

All the great spiritual teachers and philosophies encourage us to love others and abandon self-concern and yet the penny still hasn't dropped! We have pursued our own happiness all our lives and what do we have to show for it? How many things have we done for our self in order to be happy? How many relationships, how many cars, how many trips to the cinema, how many expensive meals, how many clothes, how many holidays have we had and what do we have left? Just a much bigger hole to fill inside, the more we consume or live for our self the greater our need becomes. There is a well-known saying in Buddhism that trying to find happiness in the material world is like drinking seawater when we are thirsty.

If we want to find lasting happiness and contribute to solving the problems of our world we need a completely revolutionary way of thinking and living. We need to turn ourselves inside out. Now is the time to let go of self-concern, stop being an inward-looking person and start opening your heart to others. It takes a lot of inner strength, a lot of courage and a lot of wisdom to do this correctly but it is the only way forward for us. *Human beings can't continue to live without an open heart, we will just destroy ourselves.*

We need wisdom to open our heart because letting go of self-concern does not mean that we have to run around the world doing lots of charity work, it doesn't mean we have to stop enjoying nice clothes, and evenings out and good relationships, all we have to do is change inside, become a different person within.

At the moment we probably find it easy to feel love for a few people, perhaps our close family and a few friends. But even this love is easily challenged if these people do or say something that we do not like, so this shows that our mind of love is very unstable and limited at present. But again like the mountaineer needs the mountain we need challenging people and relationships if we want to grow and perfect the mind of love. Powerful love is unchanging and stable and able to accept whatever others say or do without weakening. There are many examples of great saints and teachers from all the great religions who were able to love others even though they harmed or even killed them. We are all capable of this level of love, but of course we need to develop it steadily over time.

We can use the challenges we face in relationships to grow in our experience of love. Again we just start in small ways, the next time someone you love says something that would normally make you feel irritated just say to yourself, 'I accept this, I love this person', or 'my love is stronger than my anger' and try to just let go of any negative feeling and keep your mind focused on a good feeling towards the other person. It doesn't matter if this doesn't work at first, just keep trying and one day it will. You will find that you have developed the skilful inner ability to let go of a negative thought or feeling and replace it with a positive one.

This ability is the key to success in training the mind. Generally we tend to 'follow' negative thoughts and feelings, but this is just a habit. Because it is easy to follow the path of least resistance we are more likely to follow an old habit than a new way of thinking and feeling. So we have to expect that it will take time to cut a new path and often we may return to our old ways before the new path is complete. These small failures don't matter as long as we keep trying, it is just like losing a few small battles on the way to winning the whole war.

When problems arise in relationships and we feel drawn to arguing, our sense of 'I' or self- concern grows in our mind and we hold on tighter and tighter to our own point of view. This strong sense of our own importance is the main obstacle to developing love and having better relationships so whenever we have the opportunity we should attack it. We do this with love. *The best way to destroy anger, impatience, frustration, boredom, loneliness, or any negative mind is to just keep love in our mind.*

If you can't feel love just try to move towards it a little and keep the wish to one day have a mind of love towards others. Just that wish in itself is a special thing to have. Moving towards love might mean just being a little less angry than you normally are. It doesn't matter how small your steps are and how long it might take, what matters is that you are trying. It is when we don't try at all that the future starts to look bleak. So just try a little every time you have the opportunity, when you feel a difficult situation might be round the corner just think to yourself, 'this time I am going to react a little differently, I am going to be a little more understanding and accepting, in this way I am moving towards love'.

Remember we can't rely on others for our own peace of mind, inner peace comes from within and it is in that environment that we need to channel our mental resources if we want to solve our relationship or other problems in the long term. Of course this does not mean that we always back down or become a 'doormat', sometimes we need to be strong and firm when dealing with others, especially if we feel it will benefit them. But it takes lots of inner skill to be able to do this and still keep a good heart. It is very easy sometimes to fool ourselves and think we are doing someone a favor by telling them off when really we are just following our own selfish wishes!

We get hurt because we mentally cling on to people and things. We feel deeply that we need these things to be happy and at the moment we do because that is where we are in our spiritual development. But we can enjoy a relationship or a possession without feeling we need it to be happy. The more we let go the less we need and the purer our sense of enjoyment becomes. The way to let go is to reflect many times on the impermanent nature of things, once we start to feel impermanence, especially our own impermanence, our mind will become spacious, relaxed and content. If we can combine this experience with developing a mind of love towards others it will become very difficult for us to have relationship problems.

The essential points from this chapter are:

Our relationships are the main way we influence our world. If we have healthy relationships our life is benefiting our world. Developing a feeling of our own impermanence or mortality is a quick and powerful method to help us take a fresh look at our relationships. When we realize that life is short minor annoyances disappear and it is easier to love without attachment.

We experience relationship problems when we put our own happiness before others. If we can reduce our sense of self importance and gradually learn to love others more than our self, without being hard on our self, in time we will become a deeply content and happy person and our relationship problems will completely vanish. We can use difficult relationships to become a better person, we can train our mind and transform frustration into acceptance, impatience into patience, anger into love and resentment into forgiveness.

Exercise:

Think of someone you have a difficult relationship with, someone you dislike, or someone you would not normally like to spend time with. Completely disregard your normal feelings and go out of your way to do or say something nice to this person, even if you do not feel good on the inside, just pretend! This is an exercise in ignoring your self-cherishing mind. Once you realize that your actions do not have to be governed by your selfish instincts you are free to live your life in a very positive way.

Meditation:

When your mind has settled down develop a good intention like 'may every living being benefit from this meditation'. Spend a few minutes doing the gentle breathing meditation explained in chapter 4. Then meditate using the following contemplation:

All our relationship problems come from thinking that we are more important than others. In some ways our mental world is very small, we think about our own wants and needs most of the time and have little interest in others. Spend some time thinking about others, bring to mind their problems, hopes, worries, wishes and try to deeply empathize with them, what would it feel like to be in their shoes. This is especially helpful for solving relationship problems. When we start to empathize with others we begin to understand why they are the way they are, then it is easier to be patient and compassionate. Another way we can do this meditation is to bring to mind the problems people are experiencing in other countries around the world or the problems that animals experience in trying to find food and shelter. The more we do this kind of meditation the wider our scope of compassion becomes and the less we are trapped in our own small mind and small world. By contemplating these ideas we will eventually develop a sincere wish for others to find happiness, this wish is our main object of meditation, we should try to concentrate on if for the rest of the meditation.

When you have finished make a short dedication like 'through the power of these positive thoughts may all living beings find lasting happiness' and try to carry your positive thoughts into the rest of the day.

Use this page to make some notes on what you found thought-provoking or useful in this chapter:

8

LETTING GO OF ANGER

After reading this chapter you should be able to:
Understand the causes of anger
Identify the early signs of anger
Have practical solutions to combat anger in different
   situations

We all have an anger problem. Just because we do not go around abusing others does not mean we do not have an anger problem. We all feel irritation or impatience on a regular basis maybe even every day and these are lesser forms of anger. We could even say that the discontent that underlies so much of our life is a more subtle form of anger. So although we may not be an aggressive person our quality of life can still be seriously reduced by the presence of the more subtle types of anger in our mind. And as long as we allow them to stay the greater the danger they will grow into more acute forms of anger.

If we look at the world around us, our family and friends, people at work, our neighbors, the people we see in shops and cars and on the bus, the people we see on TV and read about in the paper, we can see very clearly that our world has a big problem with anger. People find it so easy to get frustrated and even shout at others or push past them in queues and of course much worse. Most murders occur in a domestic environment, often the final expression of years of anger, a reaction to constant abuse or sometimes just from a sudden fit of jealousy. At the lesser end of the anger scale it seems that everyone suffers from discontentment on a regular basis, just watch your own mind and those you live or work with, how often are we completely free from discontent?

The more familiar we become with discontent and impatience the more likely we are to step up to the more serious levels of anger. Discontentment can lead to impatience, which can lead to anger, which can lead to verbal and even physical violence. In this sense anger is like a sleeping giant in our mind and the more we allow ourselves to be discontent or irritated the more likely we are to wake the monster within us.

It is quite easy to see the relationship between impatience and anger and aggression, there is an obvious chain. But the link between discontentment and impatience is a little more difficult to see so we generally do not feel a need to train our mind to overcome discontentment. When we feel discontent we are usually drawn to find relief from these feelings by doing something to make us feel better. We might turn to shopping, alcohol, chocolate, we might go and see a friend, turn on the TV or the internet, anything to distract us from the unhappiness in our mind and make us feel better.

When we feel discontent inside we look for a solution outside. But the more we turn to things outside our self to make us feel good inside, the weaker our mind becomes and the bigger the problem is. Again this approach is a little like drinking seawater when we are thirsty. So if we pursue this way of living for a long time we will find it more and more easy to feel frustrated and impatient. Contentment is the opposite of impatience, when you feel content it is impossible to feel frustrated or impatient, we cannot hold these two opposing states of mind at the same time. So the more content we are the less likely we are to be impatient with others and then it is very difficult to become angry. When we are deeply content it is difficult for others to irritate us, it doesn't matter if we don't have much money or even if our partner leaves us. After many years of training, when our mind is empowered with contentment, it is almost like we are indestructible on the inside. There are many accounts of Tibetan monks and nuns who were tortured and killed after their country was invaded but were able to accept this without bitterness, some were even able to accept death and easily let go of this life because of their lack of attachment and deep inner peace or contentment.

One of the greatest contributions we could make to our world is to destroy the anger or the potential for anger within our own mind. There more deeply peaceful minds there are in this world the easier it will be for others to find that sense of inner peace and happiness themselves, but if we do not do anything and just follow our innumerable desires we are just adding to the problems of the world.

Later we will look at some practical techniques that we can use in everyday life to control and overcome anger but it may be useful now to look at how we can work toward becoming more content. Contentment means that we do not need anything to be happy, we just are. It is a well-balanced and stable state of mind that is not subject to great highs and lows or fluctuations in mood. It is an inner quality that we all need just to have a happy life, without it we are forever searching for something to fill the void or take our mind off our loneliness or dissatisfaction.

How do we find this sense of inner acceptance? Again a large part of developing contentment is learning to let go of the things that we currently need in order to feel happy. This process of letting go need not be physical; it need not involve great outer change but does involve a leap in our spiritual or inner awareness. A contented mind does not need anything but it can enjoy friendships, possessions, career etc. We can be a very energetic and motivated person and yet still be content, we can have a very successful and busy career but still be content. Being content doesn't mean that we stop living! It doesn't mean that we become introverted or full of quiet pride. Being content actually enables us to live more fully, we can engage and get involved with people and the world around us without getting bogged down in it. The sense of inner freedom that contentment brings frees us from the highs and lows of daily life and enables us to be a better person for others.

Before we can start to let go we need to realize our level of dependency and that this dependency is preventing us from finding lasting happiness from within. It is not until we start to feel that we have a problem that we will start to take this process of inner change seriously. If we want to give up smoking or any other addiction we will not really begin to try until it is obvious to us that the addiction is dangerous. The best way to get a realistic look at our dependency is to vividly imagine how easy it would be for our world to collapse even if only one or two things went seriously wrong. For example if someone close to us died or we developed a serious illness our state of mind would be seriously affected. If we reflect on this for a long time we will come to the conclusion that our state of mental health is quite fragile and vulnerable. Then we will seriously start to look for a more reliable source of happiness and protection from suffering.

For most of our life, like most humans, we have been putting all our time and energy in to developing our external environment and trying to secure our position in the material world. But because everything is in the nature of change we have been chasing an impossible dream. *We expect lasting happiness from things that will not last!* To turn this attitude around takes time, effort and commitment. We are so habitually conditioned to find happiness from outside the mind that trying to stop is a big step to take. If you enjoy shopping try not shopping for a few weeks and see how you feel, just as a personal experiment! Try stopping anything that makes you happy for a few weeks and this will give you an indication of your level of dependency and lack of contentment.

When we stop something that we enjoy we experience some dissatisfaction or unhappiness, it might feel like there is a hole within us that was previously filled with the external pleasure. Imagine giving up lots of things that you enjoy and you start to get a picture of how our mind would collapse. In this way we are not much different from someone with a serious addiction problem. The only way to solve this problem is to put some time and effort in to training our mind, developing contentment and finding happiness from within.

We can use the challenges of daily life to train in contentment. Just start small, the next time you feel you want something that you don't really need just wait a little bit longer than usual before you have it, the next time you are forced to spend time with someone you would rather not be with, don't rush off just be content and try to be friendly just for a few minutes.

Don't always be the first to push on to the train or to the front of a queue, when someone asks you for help go a little bit further than you would normally go. Generally start to take a little bit less from life and give a little bit more. It might be easy to start with because of your enthusiasm, the difficulty may come after a few days or weeks when you start to realize that it is going to take time to change the deeply engrained habits of a lifetime. So it is important to start with a realistic attitude and like giving up any addiction expect that there will be times when your mind really does not want to train in contentment but wants to take the shortest route to temporary pleasure. At these times it is important that you do not give in straight away, if you have a craving for an extra bar of chocolate just say to yourself 'OK I don't feel like training in contentment but I am going to try just for a while and then I can have the chocolate'. In this way we are putting brakes in to our usual process of behavior and this is the first way to begin changing our behavior for good.

The other important factor is that we need to be methodical and consistent and willing to push ourselves a little further when we are ready. Training the mind is a little like pushing a heavy object up a hill, if we stop for too long it is difficult to get going again and if we give up we are soon back where we started. As mentioned the best way to ensure steady progress is to make a weekly plan of action and keep a diary of your daily successes and failures and make your next plan based on your previous results. Each time you make a new plan try to set your sights a little higher, keeping in mind that your targets need to be realistic. Try to keep a light enthusiastic approach and don't take yourself too seriously, congratulate yourself on your successes, remind yourself that you are steadily building a happier future even if it doesn't feel like it sometimes! It is also very important to have friends who are trying to do the same thing and maybe a teacher who can guide, encourage and support you, see appendix 1 if you are interested in this approach from a Buddhist perspective.

In this way gradually our craving and rushing about will reduce, our mind will come more under our own control and we will start to experience moments of real inner peace and contentment. Then we will truly understand that our effort has been completely worthwhile.

Contentment in itself is enough to overcome impatience and anger. If you think about all the things that make you feel frustrated if you had a deep feeling of contentment in your mind it would be impossible for these feelings to arise. Training in patience and training in contentment are very similar. *A patient person is able to happily accept any difficulty, their mind is not disturbed when problems arise, it just remains peaceful and calm.*

This sounds like an impossible goal for us to achieve since our mind is so easily disturbed. But again it is just a matter of training, if we had been brought up in a world where inner development was valued above external development we would be a very different person now. We would be mentally and spiritual stronger and more mature, we would not depend so much on people and possessions to keep us happy and we would have the inner strength to accept difficulties without becoming unhappy. If we start to value and train in these qualities now perhaps we will be born in to such a world next time around.

We train in patience the same way we train in contentment. We already know the situations, people and objects that make us feel irritated all we need to do is make an action plan and think carefully how we can remain calm and relaxed just for a few minutes longer than usual and then over time we can build on these small successes.

Success in this kind of inner training depends upon our ability to keep an eye on our own thoughts and feelings. Learning to 'watch' our own mind is an important skill that we need to develop. This self-awareness helps us to see the chain of inner reaction we go through in stressful situations. This chain of thought and feeling has progressively larger links, and can end in feelings of impatience, anger and even violence. By learning to observe how this chain develops within us we are able to spot anger as soon as it starts to arise, which makes it much easier to let go of, and it puts inner space between us and our impulsive feelings, so we are less likely to be controlled by them.

Often impatience and anger can develop very quickly in our mind, but if we develop some familiarity with 'watching' our mind this can slow the process down enough for us to step in and change our habitual inner patterns. By doing this we also become progressively more aware of our inner environment and less caught up in the external world. Again this doesn't mean that we are cutting our self off from the outside world, in fact by developing in this way we become much more effective in the outside world, we become more peaceful, clear minded, calm, efficient and far less volatile or moody.

Watching how we act, react, think and feel on a daily basis is very revealing, almost enlightening! This is really a process of getting to know ourselves which can be exciting, scary, wonderful and depressing. Most of our life has been spent relating to others and being very involved with the 'outside' world so this inner journey can be quite daunting at first, just being alone with our own thoughts for any length of time can be quite challenging. But if we want to become happy and overcome stress, anxiety or any habitual inner pattern we need to push through this initial discomfort. Of course we do not have to do this all at once, such an over the top approach would probably put us off the spiritual path for life. To start with we just need to put a toe in the water on a regular basis and just keep living our normal life. You know what you feel comfortable with so work out a practical plan for yourself. Maybe choose one day a week that you designate as 'mind awareness day' and on that day make an effort to be mentally alert to how you are thinking and feeling, whatever situation you are in. Another good idea is to take an hour a week to mull over or write down how your mental and emotional health has been over the last seven days - you do not have to take this too seriously, don't be harsh or judgmental on yourself, just use this time to take an honest look at who you are. Ask yourself some questions, What motivates me? How do I feel and react in stressful situations? Why do I find these situations stressful? Am I happy? Am I a good person? Am I a giver or a taker? Am I making the world a better place?

Gently questioning or 'interviewing' our self in this way helps us to develop some clarity and honesty in our mind and this is a great step toward changing our inner landscape. If you want to be a little more adventurous you could even do a proper interview on yourself; imagine your life may end soon and you are being interviewed to see if you are good enough to be given more time, set out a list of tough and searching questions:

What have you achieved so far in this life?

What have you learnt and how would you do things
    differently?

What are your weaknesses?

What are your ambitions?

How often do you harm others?

What have you done to improve yourself?

What have you done to make the world a better place?

When you see suffering in others either directly or on the
    news are you moved?

Why do you think you should continue to live, how useful
    will the rest of your life be to mankind?

One of the reasons why people never change for the better is that they simply never take time to look within. Especially nowadays society is set up to encourage external development, entertainment and distraction. Why are counselors, therapists, healers and meditation classes so popular? Mainly because there is a great lack of inner peace, which comes from the lack of time we spend on healing, understanding and developing our inner landscape.

Learning to develop our self-awareness by watching our mind is a life-long practice and as time goes by we get better and better. It teaches us through experience that most of our problems, if not all, come from within. Eventually when we find our self in a difficult situation we will notice immediately that our mind is becoming agitated on a very subtle level before we develop full-blown stress, anxiety, fear or anger. Just being able to notice this subtle agitation, even if we cannot stop it developing, is a remarkable internal skill. Eventually we will be able to let go of the first signs of inner stress before they can grow in to the powerful negative states of mind that ruin our lives. To even attempt to move toward such a blissful and stable state of inner peace is very special, so many people are walking in the opposite direction to this that you can consider yourself to be a revolutionary, an outstanding individual who is playing a major part in helping humanity take an evolutionary step toward spiritual awakening.

The essence of patience is simply happily accepting difficult situations whenever they arise. This does not mean that we grit our teeth and pretend we are not impatient, it means that although we may be experiencing some problem our mind remains at peace. It is possible to keep a peaceful mind even in the face of serious problems like illness. If it was not possible, if it was beyond human capacity then all seriously ill people would be very unhappy and distressed. But this is not so, very often humans find tremendous inner strength and are able to even face death with a peaceful and accepting mind. We can all develop this level of inner peace through training in patience in daily life.

Whenever we experience small problems, like a friend keeps us waiting or our computer is faulty and we notice our mind is starting to become irritated we just say to our self, 'this is not really a serious problem, I can accept this', or 'this is an opportunity to practice patience, I accept this difficult situation'. We need to practice this over and over and become more and more familiar with letting go of unhappiness. Impatience is a form of unhappiness. We are never happy and relaxed when we feel impatience, our mind and body are tense and we can easily develop anger. So training in patience is really training in happiness. The more powerful our practice of patience becomes the deeper our level of genuine inner happiness and the better our quality of life.

But we have to accept that it will take time and commitment to progress, if we do not take a methodical and consistent approach it is probable that no lasting inner change can be achieved. Our mind is very familiar with impatience, if it wasn't we wouldn't even notice some of the minor things that irritate us so easily.

Because it will take time to let go of impatience and anger it is useful to have some mental weapons to help us cope when anger is about to arise in our mind. Of course when we are faced with a difficult situation or person that is making us feel angry one option is to just walk away. This immediately helps a potentially volatile situation to calm down and it gives our mind some time and space away from the problem so we can look at things from a calmer perspective.

Another good point to remember is that we are much more likely to feel irritated or angry when we are tired or there are lots of other things on our mind as well. Bearing this in mind it is always better to wait until you are not tired or stressed before dealing with a potentially difficult situation. This is really just common sense but if we make a conscious effort to remember this we will be prepared and more likely to have this in mind when we are feeling tired.

When someone does something that makes us feel irritated one way to calm our mind is to think carefully whether this person intended to hurt us or not. If they did not, if it was a genuine accident or misunderstanding there is no good reason for us to feel upset and just thinking like this can help us to get over it. Also we can think that even if someone did intend to hurt us it was their anger and not the 'real' person that compelled them to act or speak negatively. When anger gets into our mind it causes us to see things in a completely distorted way, it causes us to exaggerate and focus on the bad qualities of a person so that we completely forget any good times that we have had or any good qualities that they have. In this sense it is not the real person who is angry at us, they are just experiencing a temporary mental illness that is causing them to feel and maybe act negatively. They are being controlled by anger and cannot help themselves. By thinking like this it is easier to accept others' negative words or actions without also becoming angry in return.

This does not mean that we allow others to take advantage of us, it is just another line of positive thought that we can use to control and let go of our own anger. Another good line of positive reasoning is that when people are angry they are unhappy and people who are often angry are generally very unhappy people. They have lots of problems in life, they live in a very negative reality because their anger forces them to focus on the negative qualities in others, so they experience very little natural happiness or peace of mind. Remembering this helps us to feel compassion rather than meeting anger with anger.

There are many other lines of positive thought like these that come from the Buddhist tradition that can help us to find a better quality of life just by opening our mind to a new way of relating to daily problems. A very practical source book for developing this way of life is How to Solve Our Human Problems by Geshe Kelsang Gyatso, Tharpa Publications.

The essential points from this chapter are:

Anger is never useful, it only causes suffering. We all have a problem with anger, the first step towards dealing with this is to watch our mind and try to be honest about the extent of the problem. Then start to look for the opportunities in daily life to attack your anger, when you find yourself in a situation that would normally make you angry try to remain calm for just a few minutes, then gradually build up your level of patience over time. Patience is the ability to remain calm and relaxed in a potentially irritating situation.

Exercise:

Ask a good friend to insult you! Sit down together, one person tries to remain calm and peaceful and the other gives them lots of verbal abuse and tries to wind them up, then change roles and repeat. You will probably both end up in fits of laughter which is great but there is also a serious side. A sense of humor and love or friendship are the antidotes to real anger, because you love your friend and they love you it is difficult to take their insults seriously, even if they are true! If a stranger used the same words we would immediately get angry. This shows that it really doesn't matter what people say or do to us, anger comes from within our own mind, when we get angry we are actually choosing anger as a response. Although this choice might happen in the blink of an eye it is still our choice. Through training our mind we can get to a point where we always choose love, even towards 'strangers'.

Meditation:

When your mind has settled down develop a good intention like 'may every living being benefit from this meditation'. Spend a few minutes doing the gentle breathing meditation explained in chapter 4. Then meditate using the following contemplation:

What does it feel like to be angry? What are the physical sensations and feelings that arise? Try to investigate from your own experience if anger has any good qualities. Think about the times in your life when your anger has harmed others or their anger has harmed you. Think about situations you have read about or seen on TV where anger has been the cause of great pain and suffering. Based on this contemplation try to come to a deep conviction that anger is just a pointless and destructive emotion and hold this conviction for as long as you are meditating.

When you have finished make a short dedication like 'through the power of these positive thoughts may all living beings find lasting happiness' and try to carry your positive thoughts into the rest of the day.

Use this page to make some notes on what you found thought-provoking or useful in this chapter:

9

CONFIDENT LIVING

After reading this chapter you should be able to:
Identify why you lack confidence
Understand some simple methods to improve your confidence
Look towards developing a confident future

Many of our wishes and dreams remain unfulfilled just because we lack confidence. Lack of confidence is another negative state of mind that seriously damages our quality of life. It can take on different forms, traditionally when we think of someone who lacks confidence terms like shy, timid and nervous come to mind. But sometimes people who appear very confident, outgoing and bold lack true confidence. Often the people we admire for their confidence are actually less confident than us and they often use their boldness to hide their self doubt sometimes even from themselves.

Often people who are brash and bold do not have the confidence to be kind or loving or open about their feelings. In fact overconfidence can be away of avoiding deep emotional weaknesses or trauma from the past. A truly confident person is able to be honest and open about their weaknesses or strong emotions without being overwhelmed by embarrassment. ***Real confidence means having the courage to be open and vulnerable in order to grow and learn.*** It means that we are prepared to look at the weak, distorted, dark and selfish parts of our mind that most people spend all their lives avoiding or indulging. We have to develop this kind of confidence if we want to grow beyond our current limited mental boundaries.

Firstly though let's look at how we can improve our 'ordinary' confidence because this is also important if we want to have a happy life. We can see that people who have a well-balanced sense of confidence generally have a good quality of life and this is because confidence is something that colors every part of our life, it is an attitude, almost a way of life in itself. Often children have a good level of confidence and this enables them to shake off problems quickly and get on with having fun. They have a natural light mental energy that allows them to bob along like a cork on the ocean of life whereas many adults are emotionally down in the depths and find everything a struggle.

Somehow we need to recapture something we lost when we grew up. If you look at adults it is obvious that many of the problems they experience in daily life are directly related to their poor mental attitude. We often feel that life is unfair, that the world owes us a living, that others are making our life miserable, and we almost meditate on all the things that are going wrong or could go wrong. This downward spiral in our thought patterns is really the cause of most of our problems. This is not rocket science, it doesn't take a professor to understand that a positive and confident approach to life is going to make you feel good and probably going to have positive side effects. For example other people will find you inspiring, you are more likely to find employment or get promotion, you will be more able to solve problems and generate positive ideas, and when things do go wrong you will be able to pick yourself up more quickly and get back out there!

Most importantly though you will be doing the world a great service. The world doesn't need more selfish, depressed, lonely, confused, lost, anxious and stressed people, the world does need people with a relaxed natural confidence that shows others that happiness can be achieved just through changing your inner approach to life. Again, take a look at children, obviously they are not all little angels and they do have there tantrums and hang-ups but they also have this indomitable energy that keeps bringing them back up to the surface away from negativity in the mind. They have a strong wish to play, have fun and be happy and this inner energy keeps them from experiencing heavy negative mindsets for any length of time.

If we want to be happy we have to recapture our love for life, our wish to live. When we look at the adult population it seems that many people are just slowly dying. We have lots of responsibilities and life is often hard for us in many different ways and it can be difficult to be happy when we experience one big problem after another again and again. But if we let ourselves go under we have lost, we will never find the happiness we wish for if we give up, we will only experience even more suffering.

We can use our suffering to learn. The more problems we experience in life the deeper our wish should be to become a confident and happy person. We must know from experience that relationships often fail, that our health will not last forever, that money is no guarantee of happiness, yet we still keep putting all our energy in to finding happiness by trying to create the perfect external world. If we put that amount of time and energy into our personal or spiritual growth we would really happy very quickly!

Children are happy because they have an energetic, confident and happy approach to life. They do not worry too much about money and clothes and relationships, they do not take life too seriously. They live very much in the 'now', they are not hung up about the past or worried about the future and this gives them lots of energy to make the most of 'now'.

Living 'now' means letting go of the past and the future and becoming present, here, alive, full of life, full of awareness. This sense of now makes our mind very focused and powerful and confident, it feels like we are awake and alive for the first time in our life! We suddenly feel young again, our enthusiasm for life returns and little problems just disappear and we can deal with the bigger challenges much more constructively, we can still see beyond them rather than getting bogged down in them.

Living now and being fully present helps to raise our consciousness to a new level, when our mind is clear and sharp and not distracted by the past or the future we can look at spiritual truths in a new light. It is easier to feel the impermanence of things and so we can more easily let go instead of being controlled by our attachment or anger. Many of our problems come from feeling trapped in a small world and this makes us small minded and it is difficult for us to look outside and see hope for a brighter future. Increasing our confidence and energy and feeling more alive in the 'now' can help us to raise our mind above the mundane existence of everyday life and see ourselves and others in a new light.

When our mind changes everything changes. We know that when we feel depressed the world seems like a depressing, dull and lifeless place and when our mood is good it seems that the world is an interesting and vibrant place with lots of opportunities and things to look forward to. Because of this truth all we have to do if we want to live in a better world is to change or uplift our mind, to develop more confidence, enthusiasm and energy. To make this clearer in our mind, think of two people with very different personalities or attitudes. Think of someone you know or have seen on TV who is very positive, confident and energetic, think about their life and how much they enjoy it, perhaps they never feel overcome by problems and maybe even thrive on challenges. How do they see the world? Then think about someone you know who is shy, depressed, nervous, anxious and think about what the world is like for them, how does the world appear to them? It probably seems like a dark, depressing and lonely place.

So is the world we live in good or bad, positive or negative, is it a great place to live or is it awful? Now you should see that this completely depends upon our mind. In particular the world we experience depends on our level of enthusiasm for life, our level of confidence. With this in mind we can approach life in a new way. If we think about this many times eventually this new awareness will naturally cause us to take a different approach to life. It will help us to realize that trying to find lasting happiness by rearranging our external world is really a waste of time. Even if we were rich and had all the most expensive and luxurious possessions, expensive holidays, beautiful partners etc. we would not be happy if our mind was unhappy. Yet if we have a positive, confident and enthusiastic approach to life even if we are poor or unhealthy or live with difficult people we will definitely have a happy and rewarding life.

Understanding this, the first thing we need to do if we want to change is just to develop a deep and continuous wish to be more confident and enthusiastic. Partly this can come through experience, when we look back over our life and we remember all the times our mind has become depressed or anxious and how that has damaged our quality of life then this will motivate us to keep a strong wish to change. Also just watching our mind on a daily basis shows us that when our mind is dull our world is dull, when we feel anxiety our world is a frightening and disturbing place, so whenever this happens we need to use the feelings of anxiety as a mental trigger to keep developing this deep inner wish to change for the better, this decision in itself will ease our anxiety and empower our mind.

We don't need to worry, our personality or mindset is not carved in stone, it is not even a physical object. As we have already seen, even physical objects like cars and houses are constantly changing, nothing stays the same not even for a moment, we do not clearly see this on a daily basis, but this is the truth. Probably our own personality has naturally changed several times over the course of our life, so we know it can change we just need to step into the process of change and take control.

It is useful to spend some time studying confident people to try to get a feel of what their inner landscape is like, how the world appears to them and how they react to difficult situations. It is important to distinguish between people who are genuinely confident from within and those whose confidence is superficial and hides a deep insecurity or need for attention. Also we can be quietly confident if that suits our nature, because we have confidence this doesn't necessarily mean we are very outgoing or loud. *Quiet confidence can be very powerful and deeply moving, particularly in a spiritually minded person.* Often the great spiritual teachers of this world have not been loud and gregarious, their confidence is deep and stable and rooted in faith and spiritual experience. Many people who met people like Jesus or Buddha must have experienced life-changing moments because of their pure nature and confident connection with a higher force.

If we can develop a connection with a spiritual consciousness higher than our own this would be a short cut to developing all the inner qualities we would like to have, including confidence. But to do this properly we do need to develop other types of confidence, the confidence of faith and the confidence of letting go. Letting go means that we are able to be vulnerable and honest. This creates a space and openness in our mind allowing blessings or positive energy to enter our mind and touch us on a deeper level than we could achieve just through our own effort.

If we want to develop confidence, apart from receiving blessings or positive energy through prayer and meditation, we can use our present understanding of training the mind. We simply need to look for opportunities to develop our confidence. Again just take a fresh look at your life and identify the situations that make you feel anxious or worried and start trying to be confident with the easiest and work up to the hardest and most challenging situations. Make a plan, keep a record of your progress, make your next plan based on previous results and most importantly keep going, keep trying and results will come. Again this is not complicated advice, just common sense, you have to be methodical and practical, it is like going to the gym, results will only come if you keep going at a manageable but progressive pace. If you stop trying you will return to old habits so steadily build your confidence over weeks, months and years. When you feel you have reached a new level start to push a little beyond it, but don't bite off too much as this can lead to disappointment, but also don't be too gentle with yourself.

Fear holds us back from achieving and enjoying so much in life. Confidence destroys fear and that must be a good thing for our world so you can remember this too, every time you overcome fear you are doing the world a great service. There is another interesting aspect to confidence, sometimes it just comes from finding our natural place in the world, from finding out who we are and becoming content with that. If we do what we think we ought to do rather than what our heart is telling us we will never become a naturally confident and fulfilled human being.

The essential points from this chapter are:

Real confidence is not about being loud and outgoing. Partly it is to do with having the courage to be open enough to allow our natural personality to become manifest. For some people this might even mean having the confidence to be a quiet person in a loud world. Sometimes we seek company and 'noise' because we do not have the confidence to spend time on our own. A sense of confidence can protect us from problems, it can help us to shake off our mistakes and try again. Our confidence will naturally improve through training our mind. Once we realize that we have a natural source of happiness within our own mind this can make us feel confident and relaxed about the future. Over time we will develop a deep stable inner confidence based on the wisdom that all we need is a happy mind.

Exercise:

Try to find someone who has a deep natural confidence based on their inner experience of meditation or prayer. Spend some time with them and try to get a feel for where they are coming from. Then take a look at your own life and your own mind, think about what needs to change on the outside and the inside in order for you to begin to move towards your own inner source of peace and natural confidence.

Meditation:

When your mind has settled down develop a good intention like 'may every living being benefit from this meditation'. Spend a few minutes doing the gentle breathing meditation explained in chapter 4. Then meditate using the following contemplation:

Spend some time just being aware of any thoughts, emotions and physical sensations that appear in your mind. When thoughts or feelings arise try not to follow them just allow them to arise and subside like waves on an ocean. If you suddenly realize you are thinking about something, simply let it go and return to the process of just watching your mind. Eventually (maybe after a few meditation sessions) all thoughts and feelings will cease, the inner ocean of your mind will become calm and a natural happiness will arise from within, try to concentrate on this peaceful experience and 'hold' it for as long as you can. Eventually this will happen more and more and you will become a happier more naturally confident person.

When you have finished make a short dedication like 'through the power of these positive thoughts may all living beings find lasting happiness' and try to carry your positive thoughts into the rest of the day.

Use this page to make some notes on what you found thought-provoking or useful in this chapter:

10

A SPECIAL RELATIONSHIP

Lots of people have their own religion or faith or just a feeling that there is something 'out there' that is much greater than them, something beyond their current understanding. But generally we never take this feeling any further, if someone asked us 'do you believe in God?' we might say 'yes', 'maybe' or 'I have an open mind'. I think most people are like this, generally there are very few complete non-believers and maybe even in their minds there is a seed of doubt!

Whether we call this higher consciousness Allah, Buddha, God or whatever is not really an issue, what is important is that we make the most of the help which is on offer and use this to become a better, happier person. If we miss out on developing a deep relationship like this it could be the biggest mistake of our life. Life is tough, we need some help and support and encouragement just to survive. In the face of all the difficulties of life it is easy to become disheartened and cynical and our mind moves further from our potential for happiness. *When we are trying to train our mind it is a tough job without help from 'above'.*

Of course we can make progress in training our mind just through our own effort but if you have a long journey it is far easier to fly than walk and that is really the difference between working on our mind with blessings and doing it on our own. The word for blessings in Tibetan means 'to transform', blessings from enlightened beings are like positive energy that uplifts our mind and helps us to let go of bad habits and negative states of mind. If we have a strong connection or relationship with this kind of higher consciousness our spiritual life can be very powerful and we can become a source of inspiration and healing for others.

Some places have a very strong sense of holiness where you can feel blessings more easily and where your mind can be touched more easily. If you are ever in doubt whether blessings exist, just walk in to a church or temple which is used on a regular basis, sit down, close your eyes, relax and see how you feel after a few minutes. Often worries and anxieties lessen or just disappear, alternatively if you have a spiritual teacher or guide just spending a few minutes in their company can have the same effect. Eventually through training our mind and becoming more familiar with receiving blessings we can access this higher source of spiritual inspiration even if we are in the centre of the busiest city in the world. *When our mind is pure and free from negativity, every place that we visit becomes a holy place.*

If we feel comfortable with it then developing this kind of relationship is really the most important aspect of training our mind, trying to develop positive inner qualities without blessings is like trying to grow plants without sunshine! If you have ever met someone who has had a profound spiritual experience you can see that they have been touched and changed deep inside. This is really what we are looking for but in a more balanced and lasting way. We need to learn to open up to divine inspiration and be courageous enough to let go of our cynicism and pride and accept that struggling on our own is a waste of time.

Everyone is different, some people can do this quickly and easily but for most of us it involves a lifetime of steadily deepening this relationship, developing good qualities and letting go of those parts of us that make us unhappy. How can we begin or deepen this special relationship? Well, like all relationships we need to spend time listening and talking in an open and honest way. This higher energy is there all the time for us, but we need to open our heart to it and this requires a deep commitment to inner change and a sense of surrender so we can let go of pride and stop struggling alone and allow ourselves to be touched within.

Prayer or meditation is a great way to develop this close relationship but we have to find a way that works for us, one that we feel comfortable with. In some ways developing this special relationship is the most important thing we can do with our life. *Life passes quickly and what we do with our time between birth and death is a great responsibility that needs serious thought.* Human beings especially in the west have many options and opportunities to do different things with their lives, most people choose to put most of their time and energy into developing a career, having a family, accumulating wealth and so on. Very few people choose to put most of their time and energy into developing a spiritual life, yet this is what the world really needs. Of course we can still develop a career and enjoy our relationships as an expression of our spiritual path.

A human being without a spiritual life is only half a human being. We have such incredible spiritual potential, such potential for universal wisdom and love, through developing our spiritual mind we can become a very pure, kind, wise and powerful being. Yet we find it so easy to spend our time trapped in the shallow distractions of the materialistic world. It is almost as if someone has cast a spell on us to make us believe that we can find what we really want if we just keep looking outside our mind. What we really want is within us and it is the great religions or spiritual paths of this world that can take us there. All we need is to take whatever spiritual path we choose seriously and steadily increase our commitment to it over time. Then our quality of life will become very special, we will become a channel of wisdom and a light of compassion and healing for all living beings.

Use this page to make some notes about what you found thought-provoking or useful in this chapter:

INDEX

APPENDIX

Appendix 1 – Meditation

Appendix 2 – Books on Buddhism

APPENDIX 1

MEDITATION

The demand for a lasting solution to the problems of stress and anxiety created by the nature of today's 'material' society, has led to the setting up of meditation groups in almost every town and city. These groups vary in content and in their spiritual origin, so it is important to find one that you feel comfortable with, one that is run by a fully qualified teacher and one that teaches a recognized and correct 'path' true to the origins of meditation.

BUDDHIST MEDITATION

Most meditation groups can trace their origins back to Buddha, who lived over 2000 years ago. He was born into one of the richest and most powerful royal families in India and spent the first twenty-nine years of his life living as a prince. However despite having all the health, wealth and good relationships he could wish for he still felt incomplete and he could also see a great need in others for a real solution to life's problems. Finally he came to understand that most people look for happiness in the wrong place. He felt sure that true, lasting, happiness could be found simply by understanding and developing the mind. He decided to give up his inheritance and devote the rest of his life to attaining the ultimate state of wisdom and happiness, so that he could share this with others. All Buddha's teachings were recorded and passed down and to this day we have a pure, unbroken lineage of the path to full enlightenment. This lineage is now firmly established in the West. We do not have to travel far to find it.

NEW KADAMPA TRADITION

One of the largest international Buddhist organizations is the New Kadampa Tradition. Established in 1976 by Tibetan meditation master, Geshe Kelsang Gyatso Rinpoche, its purpose is "to present the mainstream of Buddhist teachings in a way that is relevant and immediately applicable to the contemporary Western way of life". Most cities and towns in the UK have an NKT residential centre or meditation group and many others are opening in the US, Europe and all over the world, (see Appendix 2 for books by Geshe Kelsang Gyatso on Buddhism and Buddhist practice). To find your nearest Buddhist centre, or if you would like a teacher to give an introductory talk on Buddhism in your area, please contact:

NEW KADAMPA TRADITION

Conishead Priory,
Ulverston,
Cumbria,
LA12 9QQ,
ENGLAND.

TEL/FAX: 01229 588533 (within UK).

Email: kadampa@dircon.co.uk

www.kadampa.net

US CONTACT:

New Kadampa Tradition

The Kadampa Meditation Center,

Sweeney Road,

Glen Spey ny 12737, usa.

tel: (845) 856-9000

toll free: 1-877-kadampa (1-877-523-2672)

fax: (845) 856-2110

e-mail: info@kadampacenter.org

www.kadampa.net

APPENDIX 2

BOOKS ON BUDDHISM

For beginners and more experienced practitioners, the following books are written by Geshe Kelsang Gyatso and published by Tharpa Publications:

Transform Your Life – A Blissful Journey

Introduction to Buddhism – An Explanation of the Buddhist Way of Life

The New Meditation Handbook – A Practical Guide to Meditation

Universal Compassion – Transforming Your Life Through Love and Compassion

Eight Steps to Happiness – Transform Your Mind, Transform Your Life

Joyful Path of Good Fortune – The Complete Buddhist Path to Enlightenment

Meaningful to Behold – The Bodhisattva's Way of Life

Guide to the Bodhisattva's Way of Life – A Buddhist Poem for Today

There are many other more advanced and in-depth titles on Buddhism available from Tharpa Publications; they also produce Buddhist art reproductions, tapes, talking books, and books in Braille. For more information visit www.tharpa.com

O

is a symbol of the world,
of oneness and unity. O Books
explores the many paths of wholeness
and spiritual understanding which
different traditions have developed down
the ages. It aims to bring this knowledge
in accessible form, to a general readership,
providing practical spirituality to today's seekers.

For the full list of over 200 titles covering:

- CHILDREN'S PRAYER, NOVELTY AND GIFT BOOKS
- CHILDREN'S CHRISTIAN AND SPIRITUALITY
- CHRISTMAS AND EASTER
- RELIGION/PHILOSOPHY
- SCHOOL TITLES
- ANGELS/CHANNELLING
- HEALING/MEDITATION
- SELF-HELP/RELATIONSHIPS
- ASTROLOGY/NUMEROLOGY
- SPIRITUAL ENQUIRY
- CHRISTIANITY, EVANGELICAL
  AND LIBERAL/RADICAL
- CURRENT AFFAIRS
- HISTORY/BIOGRAPHY
- INSPIRATIONAL/DEVOTIONAL
- WORLD RELIGIONS/INTERFAITH
- BIOGRAPHY AND FICTION
- BIBLE AND REFERENCE
- SCIENCE/PSYCHOLOGY

Please visit our website,
www.O-books.net

Let The Standing Stones Speak

Messages from the Archangels revealed
Natasha Hoffman with Hamilton Hill

The messages encoded in the standing stones of Carnac in Brittany, France, combine and transcend spiritual truths from many disciplines and traditions, even though their builders lived thousands of years before Buddha, Christ and MuhammAd. The revelations received by the authors as they read the stones make up a New Age Bible for today.

"an evergreen..a permanent point of reference for the serious seeker."
IAN GRAHAM, author of *God is Never Late*

Natasha Hoffman is a practising artist, healer and intuitive, and lives with her partner Hamilton in Rouziers, France.

1-903816-79-3
£9.99 $14.95

Is There An Afterlife?

David Fontana

The question whether or not we survive physical death has occupied the minds of men and women since the dawn of recorded history. The spiritual traditions of both West and East have taught that death is not the end, but modern science generally dismisses such teachings.

The fruit of a lifetime's research and experience by a world expert in the field, *Is There An Afterlife?* presents the most complete survey to date of the evidence, both historical and contemporary, for survival of physical death. It looks at the question of what survives-personality, memory, emotions and body image-in particular exploring the question of consciousness as primary to and not dependent on matter in the light of recent brain research and quantum physics. It discusses the possible nature of the afterlife, the common threads in Western and Eastern traditions, the common features of "many levels," group souls and reincarnation.

As well a providing the broadest overview of the question, giving due weight to the claims both of science and religion, *Is There An Afterlife?* brings it into personal perspective. It asks how we should live in this life as if death is not the end, and suggests how we should change our behaviour accordingly.

David Fontana is a Fellow of the British Psychological Society (BPS), Founder Chair of the BPS Transpersonal Psychology Section, Past President and current Vice President of the Society for Psychical Research, and Chair of the SPR Survival Research Committee. He is Distinguished Visiting Fellow at Cardiff University, and Professor of Transpersonal Psychology at Liverpool John Moores University. His many books on spiritual themes have been translated into 25 languages.

1 903816 90 4
£11.99/$16.95

Past Life Angels
Discovering Your Life's Master-plan
Jenny Smedley

Everyone knows about the existence of Angels, but this book reveals the discovery of a very special and previously unsuspected legion- that of Past Life Angels. These beings are not only here and now; they have been with us through all our lives, since our soul's creation. They are still there to nudge us, guide us and jog our memories. The clues are there, and by following them we can kick our higher self into operation, and change our lives beyond recognition.

When we connect with our Past Life Angels we no longer drift through life uncertain of who we really are and what we should be doing. Our instincts are right-our lives are unfinished business. Our soul is eternal, and has a job to do in this life. It has a master plan that has evolved through all our lifetimes.

For the first time, *Jenny Smedley* shows why your past lives are important to your future and how they can change your current one. She discusses the contracts made before this birth, both with others and yourself. She explains the illnesses and fears we suffer from, and, above all, how we can stick to the right path with the help of our Past Life Angels, once we have found it.

Waste no more time on your spiritual path, read this book and be inspired, awakened and ready to run where others walk; I wish it were around when I was ignoring those nudges and stumbling through life's lessons!
DAVID WELLS, Astrologer and Medium

Jenny Smedley has done it again and created an excellent book which helps you in this life, and the next. I work with my own angels every day but this book has shown me a new avenue to explore. Learn how your angels can hep you with your current life challenges using the assistance of your past life angels. Jenny certainly knows her stuff, and her many fans will not be disappointed.
JACKY NEWCOMB, angel teacher, columnist, presenter and author of *An Angel Treasury*

Jenny Smedley, columnist and writer, has condensed ten years experience and research into this book. A guest speaker on hundreds of radio and TV shows worldwide, she wrote it in response to the many requests she gets on how we can find that *something* that's missing from our lives.

1 905047 31 2

£9.99/$16.95

Journey Home
Tonika Rinar

Tonika Rinar believes that everybody is capable of time travel. We can access history as it really happened, without later exaggeration or bias. We can also heal ourselves by coming to terms with our experiences in past lives.

Tonika escorts the reader into other worlds and dimensions, explaining her own remarkable experiences with an easy-to-read approach. At one level the book can simply be taken as a series of fascinating experiences with the paranormal, embracing past life regression, ghosts, angels and spirit guides. But it also encourages the reader along their own journey of self-discovery and understanding. A journey in which you can discover your own connection with the Universe and the many different dimensions contained within Creation.

Journey Home offers a multitude of insights, and along the way looks at some of the fundamental questions asked by all cultures around the world. Where do we come from? Why are we here? What is the point of our life? What happens when we die?

Tonika Rinar is an extraordinary psychic and visionary, international speaker and workshop leader, with 17 years clinical experience in working with people suffering injury and illness. She has been interviewed extensively on radio and TV.

1 905047 00 2

£11.99 $16.95

Torn Clouds

Judy Hall

Drawing on thirty years experience as a regression therapist and her own memories and experiences in Egypt, ancient and modern, *Torn Clouds* is a remarkable first novel by an internationally-acclaimed MBS author, one of Britain's leading experts on reincarnation. It features time-traveller Megan McKennar, whose past life memories thrust themselves into the present day as she traces a love affair that transcends time. Haunted by her dreams, she is driven by forces she cannot understand to take a trip to Egypt in a quest to understand the cause of her unhappy current life circumstances. Once there, swooning into a previous existence in Pharaonic Egypt, she lives again as Meck'an'ar, priestess of the Goddess Sekhmet, the fearful lion headed deity who was simultaneously the Goddess of Terror, Magic and Healing.

Caught up in the dark historical secrets of Egypt, Megan is forced to fight for her soul. She succeeds in breaking the curse that had been cast upon her in two incarnations.

Judy Hall is a modern seer who manages the difficult task of evoking the present world, plus the realm of Ancient Egypt, and making them seem real. There is an energy behind the prose, and a power in her imagery which hints that this is more than just a story of character and plot, but an outpouring from another age, a genuine glimpse into beyond-time Mysteries which affect us all today.

ALAN RICHARDSON, author of *Inner Guide to Egypt.*

Judy Hall has been a karmic counsellor for thirty years. Her books have been translated into over fourteen languages.

1 903816 80 7

£9.99/$14.95

The Vision

Out-of-body revelations of divine wisdom

Jaap Hiddinga

Visions and out-of-body experiences are not uncommon, but few have been experienced in such depth, and articulated with such clarity, as those of *Jaap Hildinga*. He began to have them as a young child, and out of the thousands he has accumulated since then he presents here some of the most powerful. They range from the Christ awareness that came into the world at the birth of Jesus to travels in other dimensions, in other times, in this universe and beyond. Along the way he raises questions and suggests answers about the origins of Christianity, the nature of the quantum world, the links between the earthly and spiritual worlds, and the future of humanity

Jaap Hildinga offers no particular interpretation or path to wisdom. It is not a book on how to travel out of the body, but a record of what one person was shown when he did so. The visions are recorded as they were received. As he says, each individual can take from it what they want or need. His conviction is that they can be of value to other searchers. They changed his life, maybe they can change yours. They point to a universe that is lovingly shepherding humanity to a future that at present it can barely dream of.

Jaap Hildinga studied chemistry at university and set up a petrochemical engineering firm at Falkirk in Scotland, where he has lived for the last twenty years. In 1993 he had a revelation that completely changed his thinking and his way of life. He sold the company he had set up, and is now an independent advisor for management and export marketing.

£9.99/$14.95

1 905047 05 3